From Turban to Toe Ring

by
Dawn Devine ~ Davina
and
Barry Brown

Published by Ibexa Press

From Turban to Toe Ring

Book layout and design, Barry Brown
2011 resize and layout, Jerry Case
2011 Cover design, Kristina Reinholds
Front cover artwork, Conrad Wong © 1999
Back cover artwork and images signed "G. Helms" copyright © 1999, 2000 by Gretchen Helms.
All other illustrations by Dawn Devine © 1999, 2000

Published by Ibexa Press
www.ibexa.com

For more information about books by Dawn Devine aka Davina, please visit her website.
www.davina.us

ISBN-13: 978-0615488271 (Ibexa Press)

Table of Contents

Acknowledgments

This book is dedicated to my mother, Judy Devine. It was during the 1970s that she arrived home with her first pair of zills and practiced the smooth, undulating movements that would shape the contours of my world. Nothing in my life, especially this book, would have been possible without her constant encouragement and support.

I would also like to thank all of the people who made contributions to the production of this book. First of all, I would like to thank Gretchen Helms, whose enthusiasm for the project and artistic contributions have enriched and enhanced the flavor of the book. I would also like to thank Conrad Wong for the fabulous cover art; its quality challenged me to improve the quality of my own drawings. Barry Brown, for all of his hard work and dedication to the project. Without him, this book would just be a dream.

There are also all the people who have shaped and influenced the book in many more subtle ways. I would like to thank all of the performers of the Ottoman Traders, but most importantly, Julia "Antara Nepa" Carrol, the guild mistress and artistic director. The concept for the book was formulated when I was performing with this troupe during graduate school. In addition, I would like to thank Suzanne Dante, director of Invaders of the Heart of Davis, California. Although I was only briefly a student, it was my first taste of ATS style.

Hundreds of people have influenced my direction, clarified my thoughts and listened to me while I was going through the growing pains of developing From Turban to Toe Ring. I would especially like to thank the people who encouraged and inspired me: Pat Thomas; Nancy Klauschie; Matt and Ami Legare; the ladies of the award winning troupe Asha of Reno; that fabulous "Old Bag," Janie Midgley; Shira, Dance Goddess of the Internet; and Ian "Codrus" McCloghrie. Last, but not least, Jerry Case who spent way too much time distracting me from this project; however, I do have a higher bowling average to show for it!

Dawn Devine ~ Davina

About the Contributors

Dawn Devine ~ Davina, author, illustrator

Dawn is a seamstress, costume historian, belly dancer, and author. She currently lives in California's Bay Area. She has been belly dancing since 1985. She has degrees in Art History and Costume Design. In her free time, she collects books on costume design, writes articles for dance publications and makes costumes. Her first book, *Costuming from the Hip*, took the belly dance community by storm in 1997 and is being carried by vendors all over the world.

Barry Brown, editor, layout & design

Computer programmer by day, desktop publisher by night, Barry has been working with computers since 1976. Today, he tecahes at a local community college. His hobbies include photography (of belly dancers, among other subjects) and bicycling.

Gretchen Helms, illustrator

Gretchen Helms is a project manager at a major web portal company. In her spare time she does charcoal and pastel portraits and explored pen and ink illustration for this book. She has been dancing since 1998 and is currently studying with Davina. The two of them compose the Tiger Tribe Dancers. Gretchen shares her dancing space with a Bengal cat named Marratu who hates zills but loves to chase tassles and veils. She also enjoys photographing animals, people, and airplanes. She is always on the lookout for dragons to add to her substantial collection.

Conrad Wong, illustrator

Born in Mountain View, California, Conrad graduated from U. C. Berkeley in 1991 and has been following a successful career in the computer industry ever since. He intended to be a best-selling book author but his spare-time interests took a detour through art courtesy of *anime* and with the help of a lot of friends, has been developing his illustrative abilities for fun and a little profit. His remaining spare time is spent going "meow" at random intervals.

For more information about the author and contributors, visit the *From Turban to Toe Ring* website at www.davina.us.

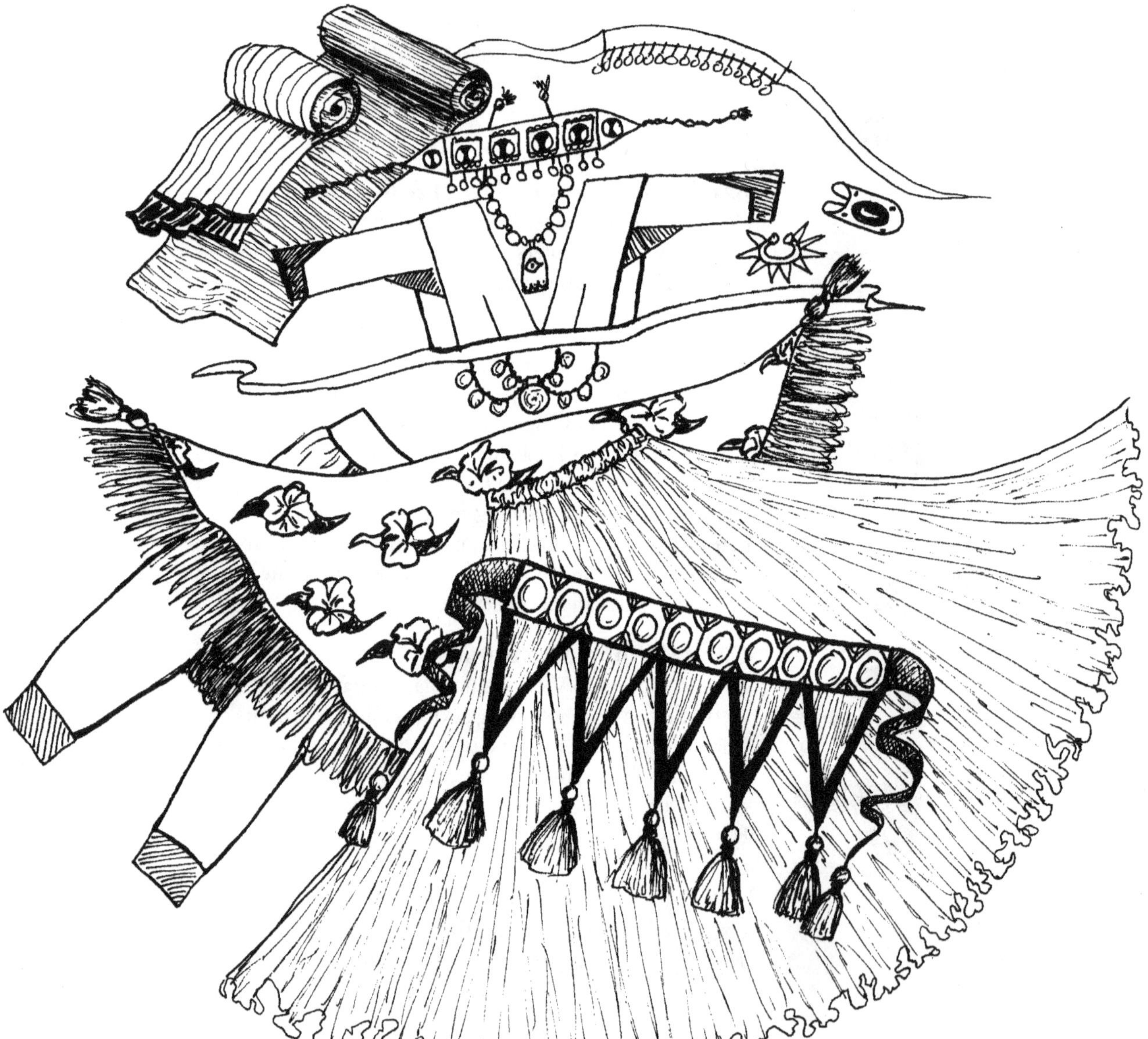

Essential costuming pieces for the tribal look.

1 Introduction

What is Tribal style?

There are many different opinions and viewpoints on this seemingly simple question. Over the years I have developed a theory about the word *tribal* and the position it holds within the world of Middle Eastern dance. For the purposes of this book, I will be using the word tribal in the broadest sense of the word. This is not a book about dance, or dance styles, but rather, about costuming and the presentation and representation of clothing from the Middle East.

For some dancers the word tribal is synonymous with a style of dance and a specific look that originated in the San Francisco Bay Area of California. It is there that dancers began looking directly to the Middle East for sources of inspiration for costuming and movement. While most dancers around the country were wearing costumes more inspired by Hollywood images and post-Tutenkammen fantasies of an imagined Middle East, tribal dancers were looking for contemporary elements imported directly from the source. They made use of imported textiles, traditional garment types and authentic jewelry.

However, the look created was a synthetic composite. Each costume was an amalgam of different design elements from a variety of different locales. So rather than wearing a costume from a particular place, they blended items from different areas. An ensemble would be pulled together from far-flung areas: a skirt from India, jewelry from Morocco, a hat from Syria and shoes from Egypt. The look is exotic, evoking the beauty of the Middle East, but is not a faithful reproduction of any specific location or cultural group.

So, for the purposes of this book, I define tribal costuming as the following:

> *Tribal costuming is a composite look created from traditional textiles and jewelry pieces produced in countries that have been touched by Islam but come from small social groups living nomadic, rural or tribal lifestyles that pull from more ancient traditions.*

This definition covers the area from Morocco to India and from Russia to Arabia. However, this does not mean that all tribal costume elements are produced by Islamic artisans and people. Druze women of Syria, Hindu women of India and Coptic women of Egypt all wear jewelry and textiles that have been influenced by Islam as a cultural phenomenon rather than directly as a religion.

For the best informatin on American Tribal Style, see the *Tribal Bible*, by Kajira Djoumahna.

Tribal does not, for the purposes of this book, refer to a particular style of dancing. There are performers who hear the word *tribal* and instantly think of the critically acclaimed performance troupe Fat Chance Belly Dance. The creator and artistic director of this troupe, Carolena Nericcio, founded her own school of American-style belly dance entitled "American Tribal Style," affectionately known as ATS. This troupe has done more to promote the tribal style costume than any other group due to their exceptionally high level of skill. Videotapes, interviews and articles in magazines and newsletters, as well as a series of workshops held around the world have brought the ATS format to dancers everywhere.

However, the tribal style of costume is expansive and reaches beyond the practitioners of ATS. Dancers who enjoy historical reenactment events, such as renaissance festivals and events held by the Society for Creative Anachronism (SCA) have created their own unique vision of the tribal style based on contemporary Middle Eastern tribal jewelry married with historically reproduced costumes. Their creations fall within this broader definition of tribal costuming due to the organic nature in which design elements from the past and from the present are interwoven to create a costume that echoes a past in which living within tribal bands was the most important lifestyle.

The Garments

How is the look created? At the most basic level, the tribal style falls into two major design groups. One style, which is most closely related to the garment styles of Pakistan and Western India, features a choli and a skirt. The other common style that falls under the tribal umbrella is the host of different, long, torso-covering garments that appear throughout North Africa and the Middle East. What these two styles have in common are the details. Both typically wear a headdress composed of either a turban or a series of scarves. They both are worn with pants and a hip wrap to accentuate movement. Jewelry for both of these styles is the same.

The beauty of the tribal style of costuming is that the dancer doesn't just have one costume with matching accessories. Instead, the performer assembles a wardrobe of costume pieces over time. Each costume is totally and completely unique due to the organic way that each wardrobe is assembled. However, a troupe can easily establish a "common" theme based upon similar cuts and fabrics used within their costume pieces. The jewelry worn by each individual dancer sets them apart as individuals while their clothing indicates their membership to the troupe. Group affiliation can also be indicated through other details such as similar turban wraps, accessories like flowers tucked into the turban and communal facial tattoos.

This book is divided into sections based on garment type and will address many of these areas. From the assembling of a "dowry," or jewelry collection, to the various styles and cuts of pants, this book is designed to define the different garment types, provide a cultural context for each garment type and give you basic design instructions to help you create them. For the dancer who wants to do further research, I have included a bibliography and throughout this book I will indicate which sources are particularly applicable to specific sections.

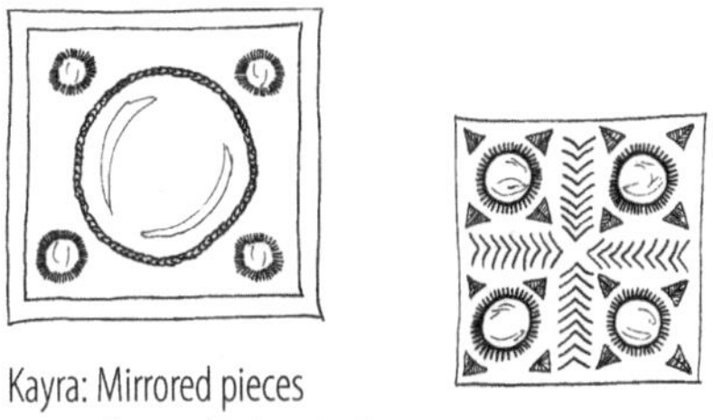

Kayra: Mirrored pieces originally attached to choil to indicate marriage.

Tribal Textiles

Many tribal dancers attempt to infuse their costumes with pieces of tribal textiles. Textiles from India are particularly important in tribal costuming. The richly embroidered and mirrored textiles produced by rural and nomadic peoples in Pakistan and the western regions of India are most prized for their exotic looks. There are several design characteristics that appear in most tribal pieces. Not every item will exhibit all of these features

Choli

The *choli* is an essential garment for women throughout India. Among tribal peoples, the choli becomes a surface for riotous color and complex patterns composed of embroidery, mirrors, shells, buttons, and appliqué. Finding a choli in good shape that fits is every tribal dancer's dream. Often, the most fabulous cholis are too small or too fragile for performance wear. Fear not, for they can be renovated and reworked. A small choli can be taken apart at the seams and the resulting flat pieces can be used as appliqués for a larger garment.

Chakla

The *chakla* is a square decorative wall hanging. They are made by young women and are used to decorate their homes. The styles of these hangings vary from tribe to tribe and they can provide a large textile surface that can be used for costuming. Small chaklas can be used as-is, merely attached to a band to wrap around the hips. Larger chaklas can be cut in half and attached to a band to create a matched pair of hip wraps. If the piece is large enough, a choli can be constructed using the square as yardage.

Above and right: two examples of chakla.

Toran

The *toran* is a decorative textile that is used in homes as a door hanging. They are composed of a rectangular frieze with an odd number of tabs suspended from the bottom. These are hung above the doorway leading to important rooms of the house. Within the realm of tribal costuming, the toran becomes an excellent hip wrap when ties are attached at either end and tassels are suspended from the tabs.

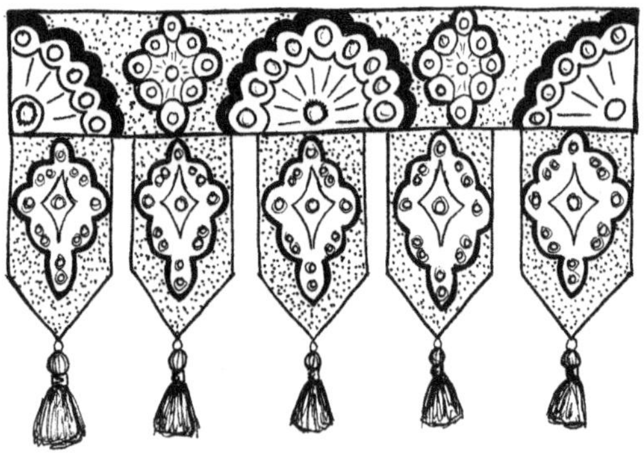

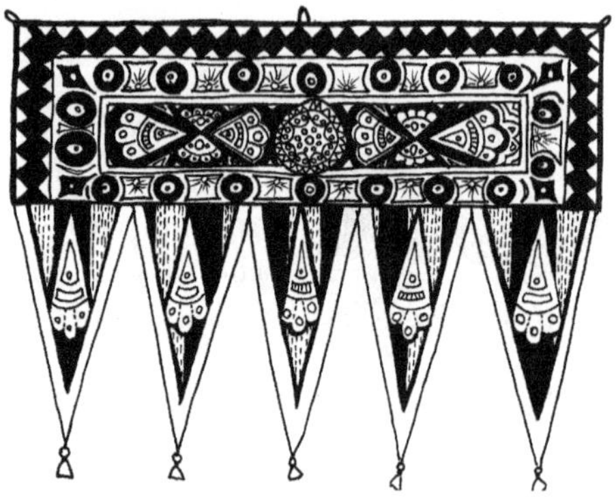

Tribal Textiles Hints and Tips

- Carefully inspect all textile pieces for loose threads. The condition of the textile will impact the price. If you find flaws, you can use them to negotiate with your dealer.
- Many textiles are fragile. Be prepared to stitch on linings or apply these textiles to a supportive base. If possible, avoid wearing these textiles against the skin.
- Look at textiles for potential beyond their original use. Pillow covers can be turned into cholis. Bags can be turned into belts. Small fragments can be combined to make larger pieces.
- Many older textile pieces are one-of-a-kind. If you love it, buy it, as you will probably not have the opportunity to buy an exact duplicate.
- Try to find out the origin, if possible. If your dealer knows the tribal group that the textile comes from, such as a Ribari piece or a Banjara piece, you will be able to seek out other items from these groups.
- Some tribal color schemes seem bright, garish or clashing to Western eyes. Shrug off your desire to match or coordinate costume pieces. One of the hallmarks of this style is the lush layering of exotic colors, patterns and textures.

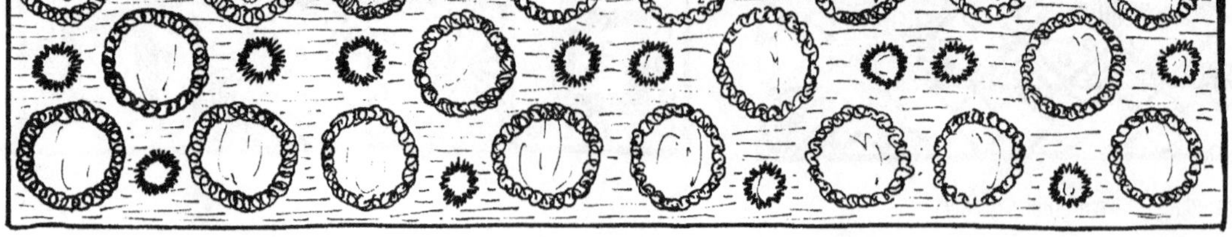

Many belts are, in reality, the ornately embroidered border of a scarf called a *mathravati.*

2 Before You Begin

From Turban to Toe Ring is a book about costume design. It is assumed that the reader is already familiar with sewing, can operate a sewing machine and thread a needle. As this is merely a single book, not every subject can be addressed as fully as I would like. Consequently, there is little detailed discussion about sewing technique within the pages of this book. Directions are included but should serve only as loose guidelines. For more detailed directions I recommend consulting some of the very good comprehensive books on the market that step you through a wide variety of sewing techniques. When I teach sewing construction classes, I always include the following books on my syllabus:

Reader's Digest. ***Complete Guide to Sewing.*** The Reader's Digest Association, Inc.: Pleasantville, NY 1995.

Holkeboer, Katherine Strand. ***Costume Construction.*** Prentice Hall: Englewood Cliffs, NJ 1989.

The Singer Sewing Reference Library produces an entire series of well-illustrated guides that are quite user friendly, including:

Singer. ***Creative Sewing Ideas.*** Singer: Minnetonka, MI 1990.

Singer. ***Sewing Essentials.*** Singer: Minnetonka, MI 1996.

Singer. ***Sewing For Special Occasions.*** Singer: Minnetonka, MI 1994.

Making patterns is not a difficult process once an understanding of the basic concepts and methodologies are explained. I touch on some simplified patternmaking techniques throughout this book. If you are inspired to read more about making custom patterns that fit, I recommend:

Armstrong, Helen Joseph. ***Patternmaking for Fashion Design.*** Harper & Row: New York 1987.

Amaden-Crawford, Connie. ***The Art of Fashion Draping.*** Fairchild Publishers: New York 1995.

Bensussen, Rusty. ***Shortcuts to A Perfect Sewing Pattern.*** Sterling: New York 1989.

Jaffe, Hilde. ***Draping for Fashion Design.*** Prentice Hall: New York 1993.

Kopp, Ernestine et all. ***Designing Apparel Through the Flat Pattern.*** Fairchilds Publishers: New York 1991.

There are also some books that will step the reader through the process of making patterns from existing garments. So, if you were to get a hold of a choli from India or a pair of pants from Turkey, you could make yourself or members of your dance troupe similar garments.

Doyle, Tracy. ***Patterns from Finished Clothes: Re-Creating the Clothes You Love.*** Sterling Publications: New York 1996.

Bensussen, Rusty. ***Making Patterns from Finished Clothes.*** Sterling Publications: New York 1985.

Selecting the Pieces to Make

There are many different parts and pieces to the tribal style. I recommend reading this book from cover to cover before you decide which costume piece you will begin first. The eclecticism of the style lends itself to assembling a wardrobe rather than designing a head-to-toe matching costume. Because of this, tribal costumes often grow organically, inspired by a fragment of cloth or a piece of jewelry. If you perform with a troupe, make sure to find out what the costuming goals and guidelines of the ensemble are before heading off in a divergent direction. This will save you from wasting both time and money.

Next, decide how you are going to utilize your time and financial resources when developing your costume wardrobe. The most expensive costume pieces to buy are the ones I like to make first. Tassel belts can be quite pricey when purchased readymade, whereas a stretch choli can be acquired inexpensively from a variety of different vendors. Look, too, for holes in your existing ensemble. Perhaps you have a number of pairs of pants but only one skirt. If having enough performance gear for several events is what you need, then having multiples in the same number might be a good investment of your time.

Some costume pieces are more versatile than others. A plain black skirt can go with nearly every ensemble and a loud print might be limiting, so put your time into developing a core group of wardrobe pieces that can serve as a base for developing a whole host of tribal looks. Beginning with a basic choli, skirt and pant ensemble will allow you to get right out there and start performing even if you haven't yet amassed a full dowry of jewelry.

Also consider your skills and the available equipment. If you don't have a sewing machine, for instance, you may want to stick to pieces that can easily be made entirely by hand, like a tassel belt. Some items, like a stretch choli, are best made on specialized equipment such as a serger. If you are a first time sewer, I recommend starting with a simple garment such as a pair of pants.

Some designers prefer to think in terms of a finished cohesive ensemble. Using a croquis to map out ideas allows the designer to consider the parts and pieces as a total look. The croquis is a design tool. It is a blank figure that establishes the proportions of the body so all you have to do is draw your costume over it. You don't even have to be an artist to use one. Just take it to your local photocopy center and make some copies. Draw your costume on and color it in with markers or colored pencils.

You can create your own croquis based on the proportions of your body. Take a photograph of yourself in a closely-fitted garment against a highly contrasting background. (For example, if you are wearing a dark unitard, stand in front of a light colored wall or vice-versa.) Using a sheet of tracing paper, trace the outline of your body. Then enlarge the tracing on a photocopier to a comfortable size to draw on. The benefit of using photographs of your own body is that you can do it from several different angles.

Taking Measurements

Many of the projects throughout this book use the measurements from your body to develop simple patterns. Traditionally, women in the Middle East have relied on older garments to use as patterns. The shapes of the costumes are quite simple, with most garments composed of squares, triangles and rectangles.

The success of a pattern relies on the accuracy of the measurements used during the pattern development. Make sure to use a cloth measuring tape to take all measurements. The tape should lay smoothly across the skin, so take care not to pull too tightly. Your measurements will be most accurate if a friend assists you. Wear either closely-fitted clothes or take measurements over bare skin for the best results.

The Sloper

There are several places in the book where I will be using a pattern-making tool called a *sloper*. In short, a sloper is a basic pattern composed of a bodice front, bodice back, a sleeve, a skirt front and a skirt back. When stitched up and fitted to the body, it creates a blank template upon which a person can design. I recommend going though this process so that you have a pattern that represents you. McCall's #2718, Butterick #5746 and Vogue #1004 are three commercial patterns that have sloper patterns with detailed directions for construction and fit. Look for them in your local fabric store. To expedite the directions in chapters five and six, you should already have made a sample sloper and fit it according to the directions included with the pattern. Transfer your adjustments to paper.

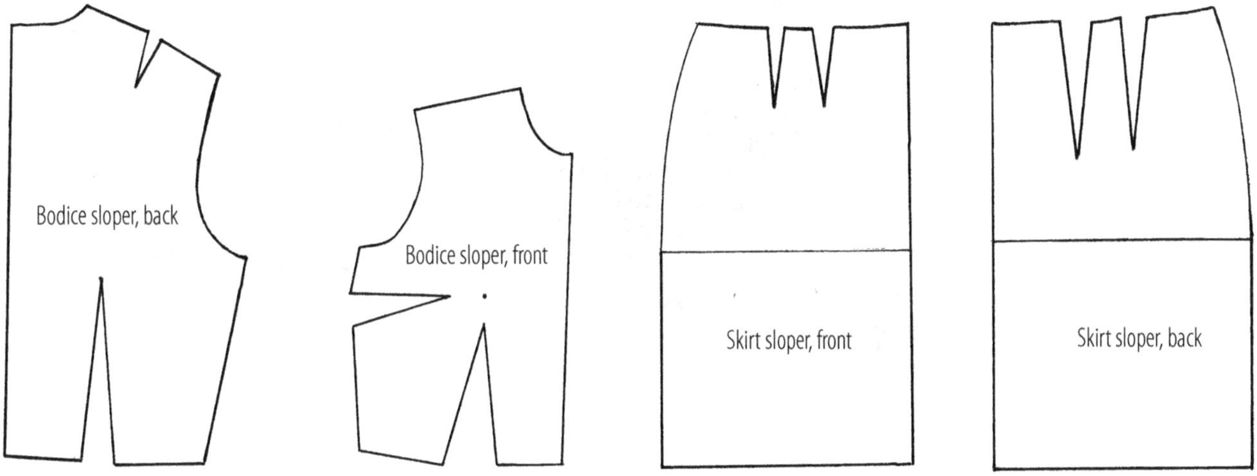

The sloper is a two-dimensional representation of the body.

G. Helms

3 Jewelry

The most impressive and distinctive element of the tribal style of costuming is the lush use of traditional jewelry. Tribal performers select pieces from the Berbers of Morocco to the Ribari of India. The adornment worn by tribal, nomadic and rural peoples continue to follow the ancient tradition of using jewelry as a condensed means of carrying wealth. Consequently, many pieces prominently feature coins as part of their decorative scheme. Most items are made from hard currency that has been melted down, resulting in few tribal pieces that, though silver colored, are pure silver in metal content.

This chapter will introduce the most common styles of jewelry worn by dancers today. Jewelry ranges in price from the affordable to the astronomical. An informed consumer is a powerful consumer. Do research on the types of pieces you are interested in purchasing so you can evaluate the condition and determine their values before you lay down the cash. Your jewelry is, without a doubt, the largest investment you will make in your tribal ensemble.

Creating a Dowry

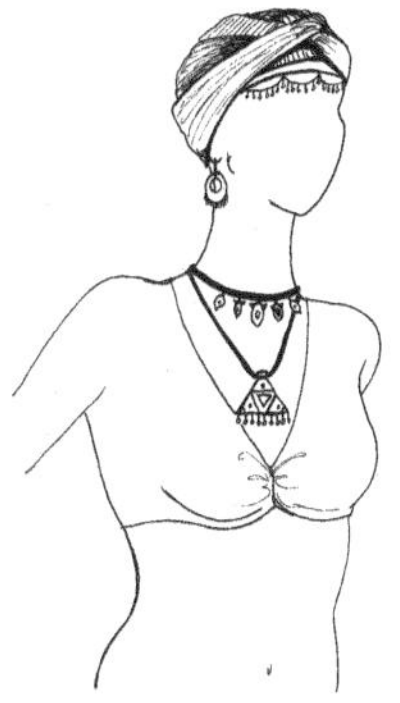

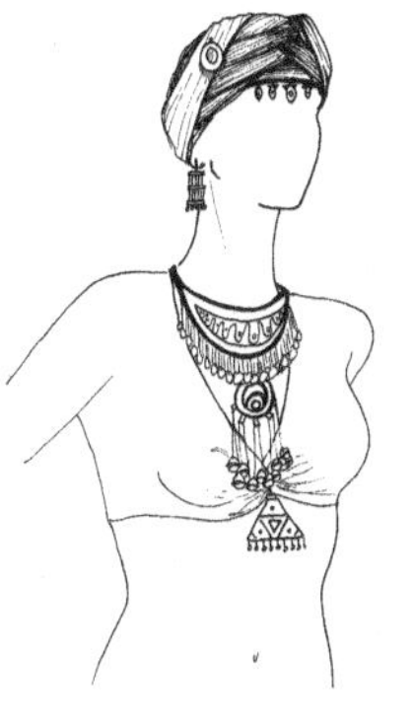

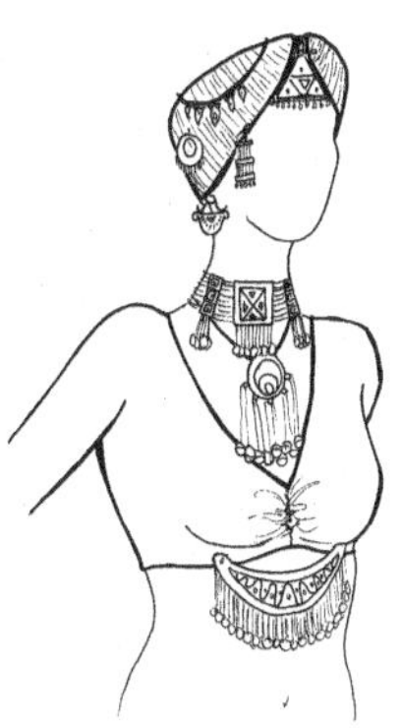

As you build a wardrobe of costuming pieces, experiment with their position and placement.

Jewelry is expensive and purchasing a complete ensemble at one time could cost hundreds, if not thousands, of dollars. In tribal societies, a woman's dowry is accumulated by her family starting at a very young age. Her collection is then amended after her marriage by her husband and his family. Putting together a "dowry" from scratch can be a daunting project. Financially, it represents the largest expense of putting together a tribal costume. Pieces have to be sought out, evaluated for quality and then purchased. It's a treasure hunt of sorts that can take you from antique stores to flea markets, from your favorite dance vendor to local bead shops and import stores.

With an entire wardrobe to build, where does one begin? That's a good question and one that is not easily answered. A dancer must weigh several issues when assembling her jewelry pieces. Budget is probably the most critical limitation that dancers face. Establishing a budget is the first step towards assembling a tribal jewelry wardrobe. Each dancer must determine how much of a financial investment she is willing to make towards creating her "look." A fabulous ensemble can be created at practically any price and, frequently, money can be saved through careful hunting and by filling the ensemble in with tribal-flavored pieces, reproductions and "filler" jewelry such as beads and shell necklaces.

Next on the list of considerations is availability. Finding tribal pieces can take time, effort and patience. Some dancers initially will purchase any pieces they can afford, banking on the notion that they will be able to resell or reuse items in new ways. In some areas, tribal jewelry is such a rarity that making purchases via mail order or the Internet becomes the only practical way of acquiring desirable pieces. Remember, you may wind up purchasing a few necklaces and pairs of earrings before you find the perfect bracelet that fits. Or you may start out small, with parts and pieces that can be simply strung on cord.

Styles and Countries of Origins

While this book does not have the scope necessary to discuss with detail the nuances of tribal jewelry, a basic understanding of the different styles is essential when shopping. Knowing the country of origin and the quality of the piece will give you bargaining power when you are purchasing items. This is especially important when you are shopping antique stores, resale shops and at flea markets, where the persons selling the goods may not know, themselves, exactly what they have. Be aware of what market prices are like. Comparison shop the dance supply vendors in your area, online and at dance events to get an idea of current prices.

While the main focus of this survey is upon rural or tribal jewelry style, do not hesitate to blend rural with urban styles. India, to use an example, has a long tradition and complex cultural practices involving the display of jewelry. Each major region of India has its own styles, media and techniques. Subsequently, there are many subtle permutations that would effectively enhance the dowry of a tribal dancer.

Turkomen

The jewelry of the Turkomen tribes is very distinctive. These nomadic people of Central Asia have a metalworking tradition whose roots lie deep in the mists of the past. Pendants in different sizes and shapes, plaques that are worn either as jewelry or stitched onto their garments and bracelets are available in the costume market today. Although there are several major tribes, most jewelry available comes from the Tekke tribe.

There are several highly distinctive features of Turkomen jewelry. Pieces are typically composed of broad expanses of metal—usually silver—that are gilded in patterns across the surface. Carnelian bezels break up the overall surface design of most Tekke pieces. There are many motifs taken from nature that have been stylized, such as rams horns, and are believed to have talismanic properties of healing and protection. Preferred shapes for Turkomen jewelry include triangles, squares and diamonds embellished with sinuous curving lines.

Bracelets or Bizelik

These cuffs are very distinctively designed. They are made in a solid piece, with the arm slipping through an opening at the side. Stylistically, they are composed of regular bands or units that wrap around the wrist. Raised strips of gilded metal delineate the segments on the cuff. Cuffs come in multiple bands with as many as seven segments and they are typically made and worn as a set.

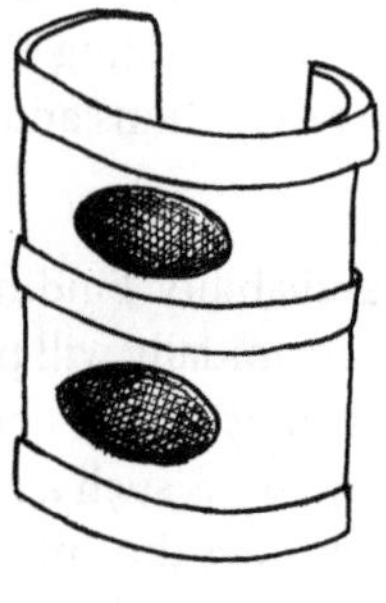

Carnelian bezels provide color and decorative embellishment in Turkomen jewelry.

Pendants

For Turkomen women, the chest is a surface for the complex display jewelry. Pendants come in all sizes from the large *gonzuk*, covering most of the chest, to elegant pairs of *tenechir*, hanging in pairs from the temples. *Bukov*, or necklaces, are generally worn with a central medallion or plaque in geometric patterns, such as squares, rectangles and diamond-shaped lozenges. Frequently, pendants worn by Turkomen women as hair ornaments, such as an *asyk*, are worn by dancers on a chain around the neck.

Asyk pendant

Turkomen pendant

Bukov necklace

Moroccan

The Berber peoples of Morocco and across North Africa wear jewelry starting from their early childhood. Women assemble their dowry from parts and pieces that they collect, are given or are recycled from older ensembles. Three of the most distinctive styles of jewelry worn in Morocco are the assemblage necklaces, the fibula used to hold together their wrapped garments and the wearing of talismanic amulets, of which the hand of Fatima is the most important.

Fibula or Tizerzai

The Berber people traditionally wear one of the world's oldest styles of dress. Imported from Greece as early as 600 BC, the wearing of a wrapped garments date back to the early settling of the area by the Greeks and, subsequently, by the Romans. The word *fibula* is Roman and refers to the pair of large pins that were used to hold the wrapped garments closed. They are worn at both shoulders and are often connected by a length of chain. Amulets and other decorative elements are frequently suspended between pairs of fibula.

The fibula is one of the most utilitarian pieces of Moroccan jewelry. It is composed of a pair of pins with a large field of metal upon which to embellish using elaborate jewelry-making techniques. They can be geometric shapes, of which triangles are most favored for their reference to female fertility. Other forms are stylized images from nature and often feature amuletic imagery.

Hand of Fatima — Khamsa

The hand of Fatima, daughter of Mohammed, is a very powerful amulet across North Africa. Representations of Fatima's hand have long been cherished for their ability to ward against the evil eye and protect the wearer from harmful spirits. These amulets can appear almost anywhere in a woman's jewelry ensemble and vary in size from tiny charms to large medallions. They can vary in shape as well, from stylized geometric forms to representations of an actual hand. Frequently an eye appears in the center of the palm, a secondary amuletic property that further protects against the evil eye.

Assemblage Necklaces or Tachroucht

Tachroucht are elaborate multi-stranded necklaces that are composed of numerous different elements. These pieces are large and substantial and can come in many different lengths from nearly a choker to hanging down to belly button level. Each woman either creates her own, or her husband has his female family members create one for her. They frequently are composed of parts from older pieces that have been recycled.

The most common elements to find worked into assemblage necklaces are coral, amber, glass beads, sea shells (including cowries, slices of conus and limpets), copal, lapis, carnellian and amazonite. A variety of amulets called *tachbats* are also included, as well as coins and metal beads. Amulets can feature such symbols as turtles, salamanders, jackle paw, crosses and solar motifs that protect against a variety of evil spirits. However, the most striking

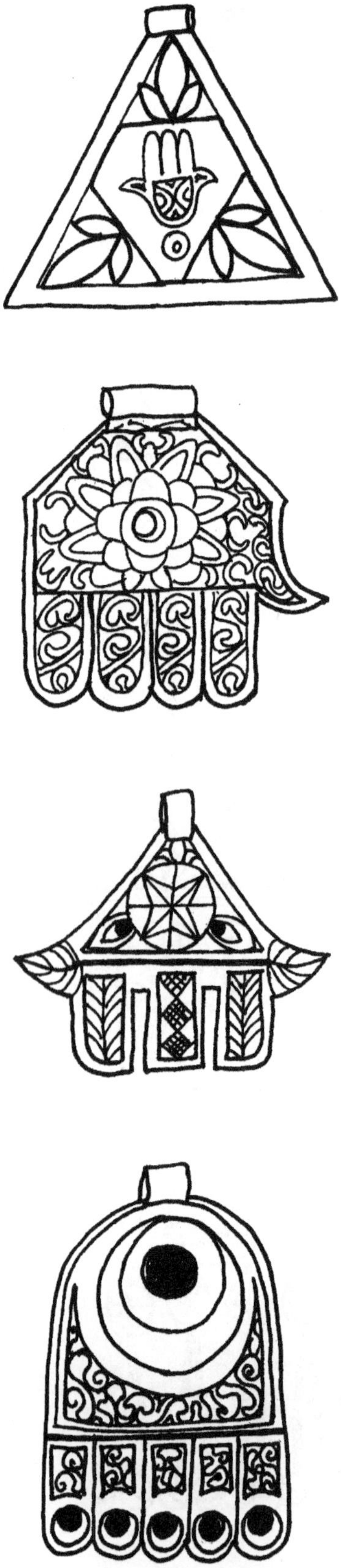

Hands of Fatima (Khamsa)

and distinctive element of these assemblage necklaces are the elaborate cloisonné eggs called *tagemout*. These fertility symbols appear in odd numbers in these necklaces and often have coins or bells dangling from them. Other major pieces that can be incorporated into the assemblage are Koranic boxes which contain verses from the Koran. Large *khamsa* can appear at the center of tachroucht as well.

Berber fibula with tagemout

Assemblage necklace with prayer case

Arabian/Afghani

Qiladeh necklace

Without a doubt, the largest proportion of tribal jewelry available from vendors today comes from Afghanistan and Pakistan. These pieces come from an assortment of tribal groups, although most come labeled as Kutchi Tribe. These pieces come in a wide assortment of shapes and sizes but with some characteristic features that are found in jewelry throughout Arabia, Syria and across the Middle East as far as India.

These pieces are, in general, made of coin metals set with glass or semi-precious stones. Geometric shapes are preferred and there are frequently a series of drops or smaller pendants integrated into larger pieces. Metal balls, coins and bells add movement and noise.

Chokers

As the jewelry item of choice for most dancers, these can be a very expensive investment. Finding one that is intact, with all of the drops and stones in place, can be challenging. Reproductions of these types of chokers can be an inexpensive way of achieving the look without the expense. But these reproductions fail to capture the weight and substance of the real article. These chokers can be used not only around the neck, but as a stomach drape or, if you have a pair of similar items, mounted onto a bra.

Pendants

These are probably the most common jewelry component available from vendors. These come in all sorts of sizes, as small as a single coin with a gem mounted on it or large enough to cover the entire chest. Small pendants can be stitched onto bras or belts, pinned onto turbans or incorporated into larger necklaces. Large pendants can be transformed into the centerpieces of necklaces, pinned onto the bra or choli as a stomach drape.

Necklaces or Qiladeh

Arabian and Afghani necklaces are frequently mounted directly onto black braided cord. These feature pendants which hang down in odd numbers surrounding a larger central stone medallion. There is a tremendous variety in the styles of necklaces in construction and materials. They can feature coins set with stones or have specially constructed drops. The pendant drops may have layers of smaller drops or have metal bells suspended in a fringe.

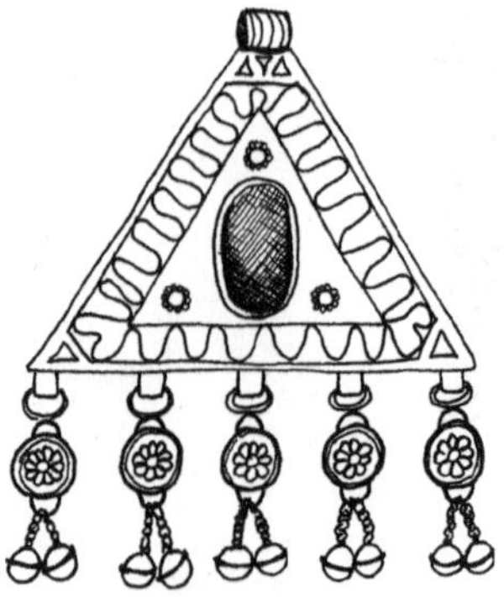

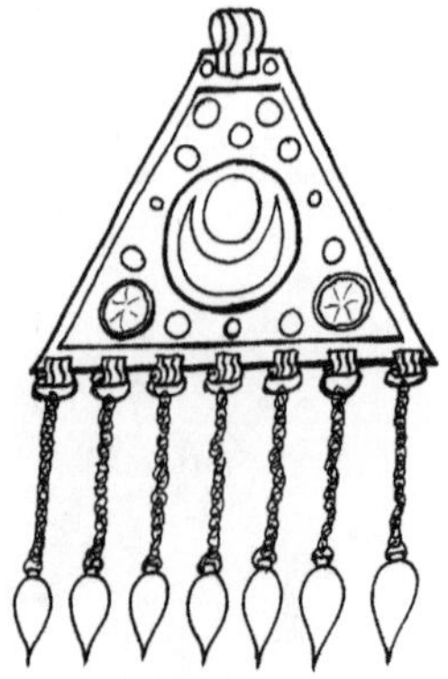

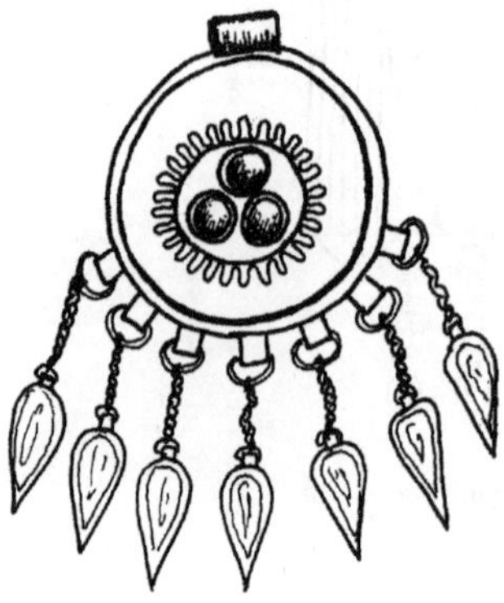

Above and right: small pendants for use as turban decorations, bra embellishments or belt accessories.

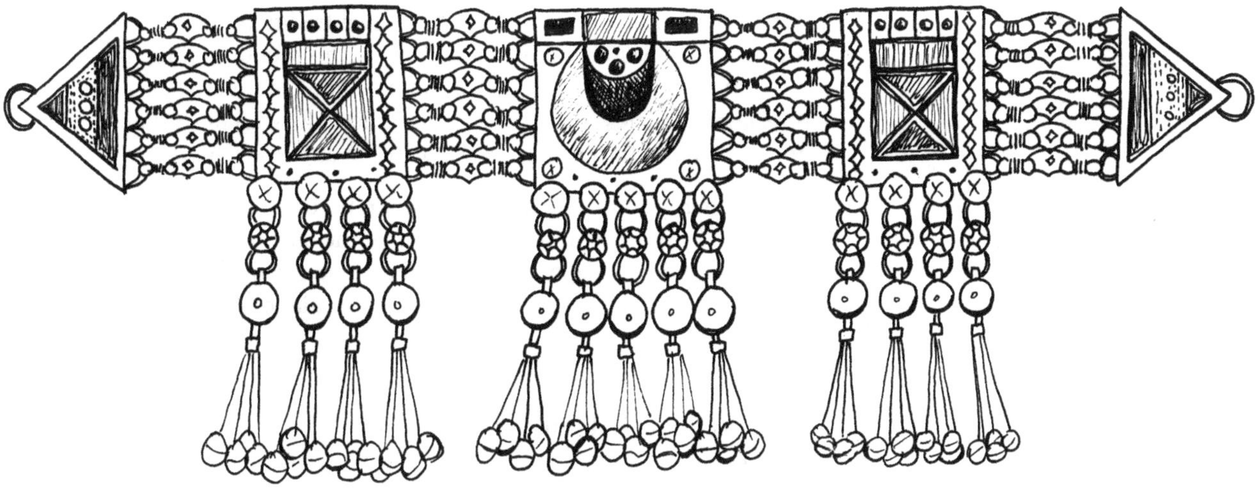

Afghani choker

Afghani necklace

India

There is a tremendous variety and scope to the jewelry production of India. Each district and major city has its own traditions and styles. Rather than trying to cover all of the different types, this section will focus on the jewelry of rural peoples such as the Lambani and the Ribari, gypsy tribes whose jewelry shares more in common stylistically with the ornamentation commonly found further west in Afghanistan and Pakistan.

From her headdress to her toe rings, no part of the female body is left unadorned by jewelry in India. It is law that the only property a woman can own is her jewelry. Consequently, in the quest to develop her value and wealth, women will invest and wear large quantities of jewelry.

Nose ring

Nose Rings

One of the most distinctive features of the complex Indian jewelry ensemble is the use of the nose ring. While you may not have your nose pierced, these rings can look fabulous when pinned on the turban as a centerpiece or when worn in a pair as earrings. These are generally either set with glass pieces or with rows of tiny dangling balls or bells.

Bracelets

Many huge, dangerously-pointed bracelets are worn by the tribal women of India as protection and as a visual statement about the strength and power of the tribe. These bracelets can send the same message here and can add a dramatic power to any tribal costume. Other women wear rows and rows of bracelets up and down the lengths of their arms from their wrists as far as their elbows and beyond.

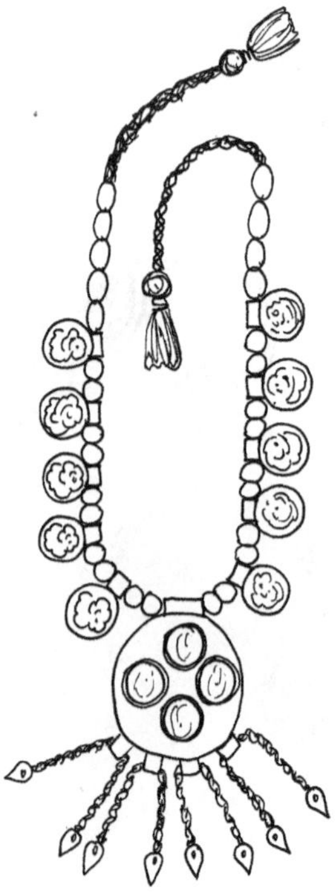

Inexpensive Starter Jewelry

Many vendors carry starter jewelry for Middle Eastern dance. Made from white- or gold-toned soft metals, these items are inexpensive and readily available. From anklets composed of a length of chain with bells to belts composed of swags of chain, coins and bells. While these are great to begin with, they are not really tribal in style or sturdy enough to stand up to the rigors of dance.

Some tribal dancers, though, wear Indian-made bra covers over stretch cholis. This can produce a very nice look that will survive the rigors of performance, especially if they are mounted onto a bra base. That supports the piece and prevents the soft metal jump rings from pulling apart.

Russian box

Other Regional styles

There are numerous other jewelry styles that can blend, mix and augment the tribal look. So many, in fact, that it is nearly impossible to touch on all of them in one small chapter. However, keep your eyes open to possible additions from unusual places. Ancient Egyptian beaded collars can form a nice base for the overlaying of more current tribal styles. Some African designs will blend in seamlessly with tribal costumes, such as the pendants worn by the Tuareg. Some pieces from further east, such as Tibet and Nepal or Hill Tribe jewelry, will provide a good source of pendants and wrist cuffs. Even some Native American silver jewelry inlaid with stones will integrate into a tribal ensemble.

Tuareg cross

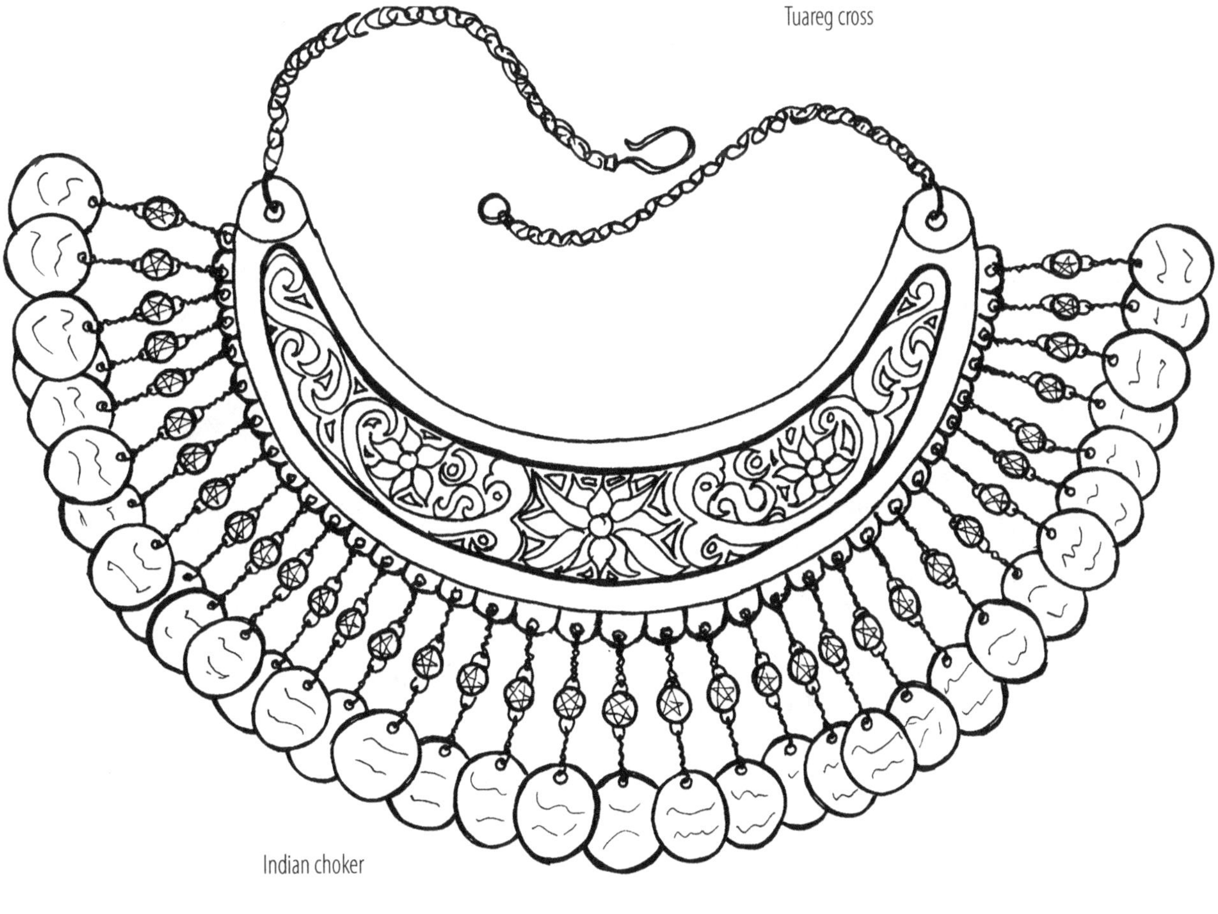

Indian choker

Buying Jewelry

- Buy pieces you like! If you don't love a piece, let it pass. If it's an outrageous deal, then by all means pick it up for future trading or gift-giving.
- Purchase only what you can afford. Make sure to set a budget. Tribal jewelry prices vary wildly from dealer to dealer.
- Shop around. Sample the wares of as many different vendors as you can. When you find a dealer who carries merchandise you like, establish communication with them and let them know what you are looking for. Competition is fierce, so often times dealers will work to maintain a loyal customer base.
- Have a wish list. Have an idea of the pieces that you want to buy. Let your friends and family know what types of pieces you are interested in, for those potential gift giving moments.
- Keep parts and pieces for repairs. Have pieces that are missing a few dangles? Missing stones? Don't get rid of them. Some jewelry can be restored with the use of jump rings and some leftover or broken pieces of jewelry.
- Look past any dirt or grime. Jewelry pieces can be cleaned. Some jewelry, however, uses wax to hold the stones in place. When you are shopping, inspect your pieces closely to determine how much of the grime can be safely removed. And remember, as some vendors will charge less when the jewelry is dirty, you could reveal a diamond in the rough.

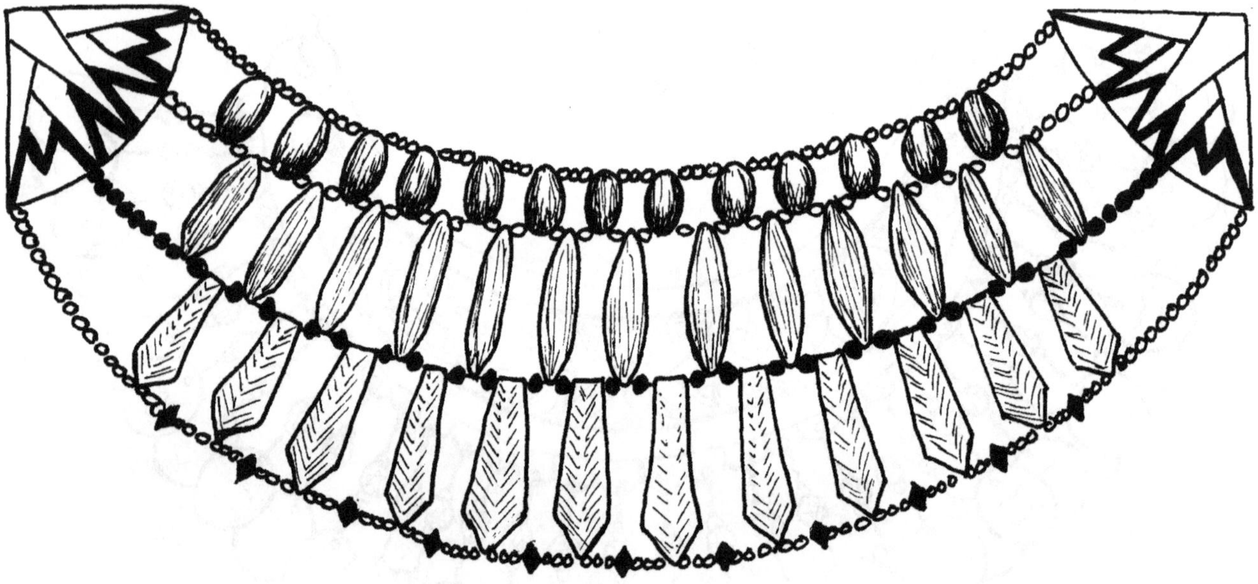

Ancient Egyptian beaded collar.

4 Head Wear

The turban is, perhaps, the most distinctive element of the tribal ensemble. It rests on the head of the performer like a crown, giving the dancer a regal and elegant bearing, increasing her height and adding to her presence on stage. The turban becomes a focal point for displaying jewelry, providing a base upon which to pin almost anything from pendants to nose rings and can be draped with beads, necklaces, pearls or shells.

Of all of the parts of the tribal look, the turban is the most fantastical. Appropriated from the Middle and Near East, this garment is typically worn by men. Women in most tribal societies from Morocco to India wear an assortment of headgear from scarves to hats. It is only in the desert dwelling societies where the turban is acceptable attire for women. The turban, however, is so closely associated with this geographic region, that it almost serves as a code, becoming an emblem for a far distant culture rather than a representation of its actual cultural practices.

However, the turban is an excellent choice for the performer. Unlike a complex layering of scarves, the turban can be tied tightly to the head, allowing a full range of arm motion. The added benefit is that the back of the neck and upper torso are kept bare, adding to the long, lean, elegant line of the costume and allowing the audience to see the back of the choli. Many dancers who enjoy a more covered look will wrap and pin a veil to their turban as a final layer of costuming. In either case, it is the turban that serves as the headwear of choice for tribal dancers.

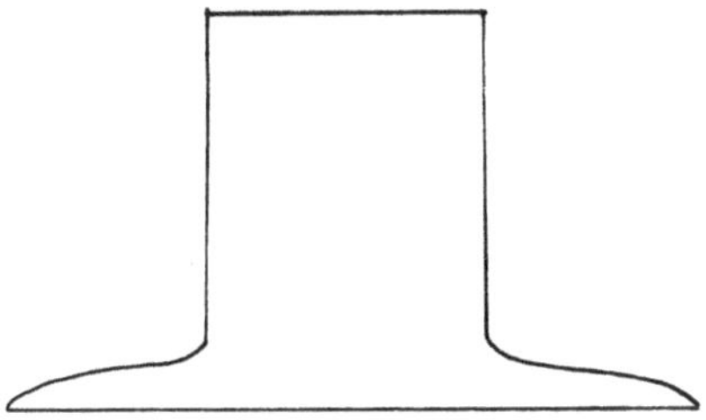

Turban Materials

There are two main parts of a basic turban: the base and the turban cloth. Some dancers prefer to start with the turban cloth directly on the head, but for security, a base cloth provides a level of tooth and grab and helps to compensate for the smoothness of hair. The base can be as simple as a cotton bandana folded in half and tied over the head at the base of the neck. More complex versions can be constructed by simply making a rectangle that reaches across the head behind the ear on either side, extends over the back of the head and, if you desire, down the back of your neck. Tabs for tying can either be made out of the fabric or applied as a band across one end.

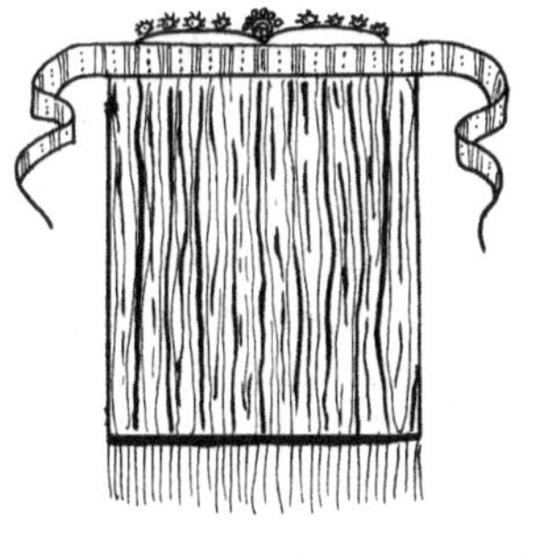

There are many ways to decorate your turban beginning with the very first layer.

The base cloth can form the first layer of decoration. A band of jewelry can be applied permanently across the front of the headdress to hang down over the forehead. This could be composed of any number of elements. It can be adorned with something as simple as an inexpensive anklet from India, or can be as complex as a series of coins, jewelry pieces and shells. Some necklaces work perfectly for this type of embellishment and can be stitched on quickly to create a stunning effect.

The rest of the turban is composed of layers of narrow fabric twisted, wrapped and knotted around the head. A few simple techniques can create

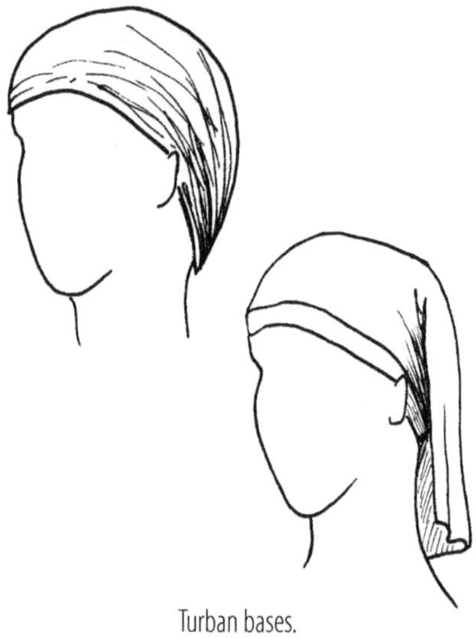

Turban bases.

an almost infinite number of possible turban shapes. The ultimate look will be determined by the width, length and thickness of the turban cloth. There are no finite rules for determining the ideal length of fabric for a turban. Ideally, investing in some lengths of inexpensive yardage to experiment with will allow you to experiment with different lengths and widths. If you know someone who is an accomplished turban wrapper, they will be an invaluable source of information and may have turban cloths for you to experiment with before you make the financial investment of a costly length of fabric.

In general, you will need enough yardage to completely wrap around your head a minimum of three times with enough left over to tuck into the turban securely. Turbans vary in width from as narrow as four inches to as wide as eight. The thicker the fabric, the shorter the length needed. Therefore, if you are using a very finely woven cloth, a longer length will be needed to build up a nice substantial base. Cloths with large all-over patterns will appear to be larger; complex subtle designs will give a more sumptuous look. A good starting point is a turban that is 6 inches (15 cm) wide by 3 yards (1 m) long.

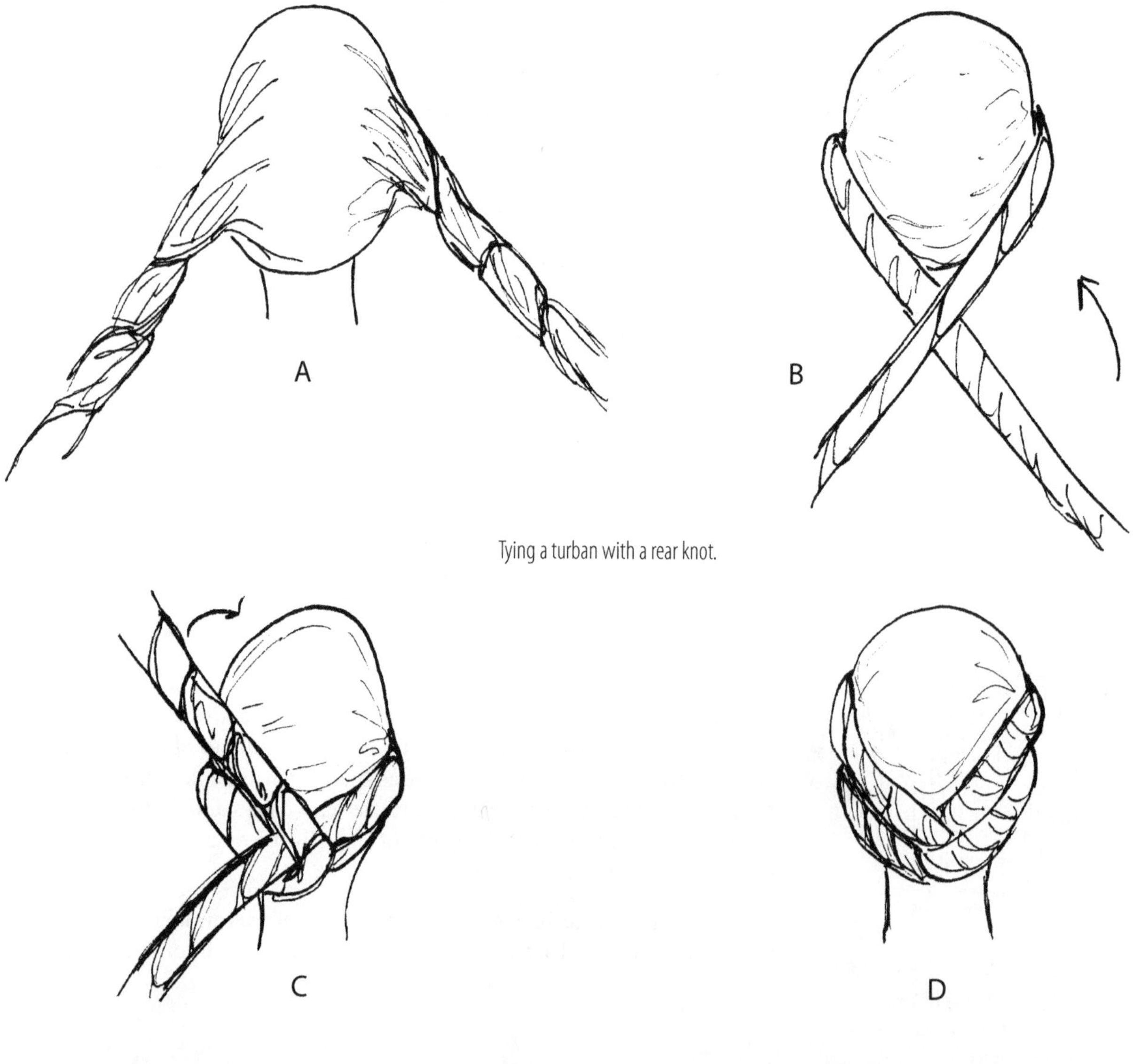

Tying a turban with a rear knot.

Tying the Turban

There are many ways to tie a turban. The final look of the turban will depend on the length of your cloth, the heaviness of the fabric and your wrapping skill. The turban cloth can be twisted as you wrap, or can be wrapped flat creating a smoother shape. Experiment with variations on these themes.

There are really only three basic turban styles. The first is to begin from one end of your turban cloth. The turban is wrapped in one direction around the head. The other two methods involve placing the turban cloths centered on the head. From there, the ends are either wrapped to the front, knotting above the forehead, or wrapped towards the back. These are definitely techniques that gets better with practice and is much easier to learn them first-hand in person than through the pages of this text. I have put together a few simple steps to get you started wrapping.

Top knot, step 2

Top Knot

Step 1: Tie your base cloth firmly onto your head.

Step 2: Place your turban across the top of your head so that the two ends hang down. Or, if your cloth is too narrow, you can start with it centered at the base of your skull. Twisting slightly, take either end and pull to the front.

Top knot, step 3

Step 3: At the center of your head, just above your forehead, overlap the two ends.

Step 4: Twist the two ends and pull to the back of your head.

Step 5: Wrap the ends around the back of your head and bring to the front.

Repeat this procedure until you have built up the knot in front to the size you desire. After the first knot, you can just continue to wrap the turban around smoothly to build up the size of the turban. The directions for a rear knot version are essentially the same, only you are tying in the back of the head under the occipital bone.

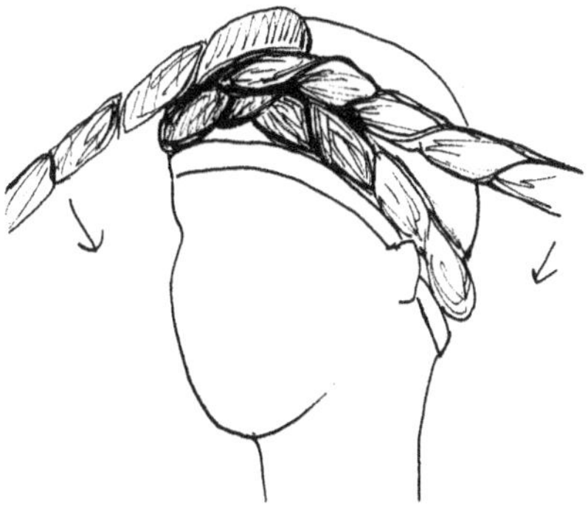

Top knot, step 4

Multiple cloths can be twisted together for a colorful turban.

Decorating the Turban

Once the turban is in place, it becomes the foundation for the display of wealth. Some dancers heap the jewelry on, layering it thickly with a wide assortment of tribal pieces. Pendants, drops, earrings, nose rings, chokers, necklaces and even anklets can be used to decorate the turban. When in doubt, try it! Experiment with all of the pieces of jewelry you possess to find the look that is most advantageous for your face and favored turban shape.

Jewelry is pinned into place using long corsage pins available at florists and in craft centers that carry silk flowers. Also, many vendors who carry tribal supplies will have these pins, which look like overgrown sewing pins with large, often pearlized heads. Hatpins can be found in some hat stores that have beautifully jeweled and embellished heads on them which can be incorporated into the tribal ensemble. These pins can be treated creatively. They can be painted or wrapped with metal. The adventurous and crafty can remove the head and glue a bead in its place. Be careful not to stab yourself trying to peel off the heads!

There seem to be some common ways of wearing jewelry on the turban. Below is a list of some ideas to get you started. Nothing, however, will replace experimentation and play. Also, don't forget those older pieces that you may have languishing in a box because you have upgraded your jewelry. Since almost any piece can be integrated into the turban, your imagination is limited only by the increasing weight as you heap on the jewelry. Described below are some good places to put jewelry.

Across the Forehead

From Morocco to India, Turkey to Yemen, women wear a band of jewelry across their forehead. When you wear a turban, this area is a wonderful place to stretch a necklace, a soft anklet or bracelet. In many areas, a row of coins will be integrated into a woman's headdress. A band of coins can also be worked into the wrappings of the turban. A headband of coins will allow you to achieve the same look over and over again, rather than pinning individual coins to your turban for each performance.

Center Front

One large medallion, pendant, or pin will make a striking centerpiece for the turban. Look at your jewelry in a new way. Some necklaces with a large, central medallion can be draped in a swooping manner across the crown of the turban. This can be a single large necklace or it can be a series of smaller necklaces that fall in a cascade as they wrap around the turban. Also think outside of the box: shells, stones, beads and coral necklaces can be as effective as metal jewelry pieces.

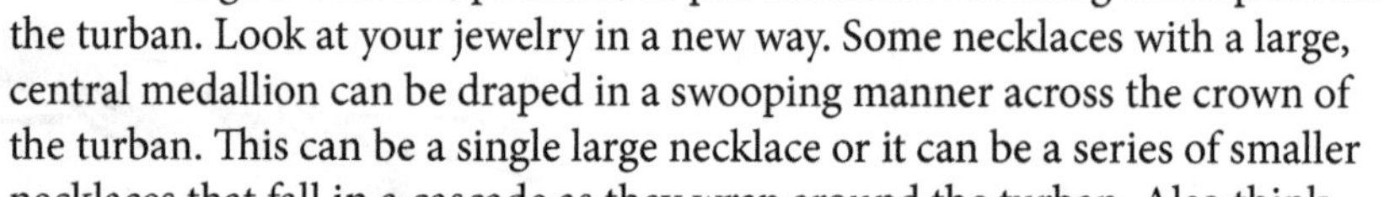

Stitching decorative headbands together will reduce time when putting on your turban

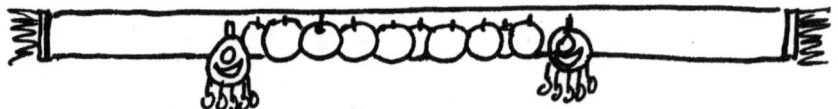

Draped Down the Side of the Face

Some dancers wrap up their ears completely when they tie their turban. Consequently, earrings may not be an option. Don't let this be a barrier for the dramatic display of jewelry that drapes down the side of the face. Earrings or pairs of matched pendants can be pinned onto the turban beside the face to drip down. This is an excellent way to wear a pair of fibula from Morocco.

Everywhere Else!

Ultimately, only the contents of your jewelry collection will determine what are the best places on your turban to display them. When shopping for jewelry, know where there are empty spots in your favorite turban wrapping so you can purchase accordingly. Also shop in your own collection. Shift jewelry around and experiment. Move things around and mix it up until you find the look that is totally you.

Hats

Some dancers prefer to let their hair show and choose to wear hats rather than a turban. Shopping for a hat or headdress of this type can be a little more complicated than putting together a turban. Hats are more difficult to make, although you can find simple pill box shapes in the pattern collections of all the large pattern-making companies.

If you are making a hat, make sure to use a firm base. Plastic needlepoint canvas makes a nice firm base upon which to hang jewelry. If you are purchasing a hat, make sure to try it on and dance in it. Some hats look wonderful but don't really fit well. If this is the case, and you love it, try wearing it with a narrow turban around the base of the hat to hold it on the head. This look was quite popular among Ottoman ladies for many centuries.

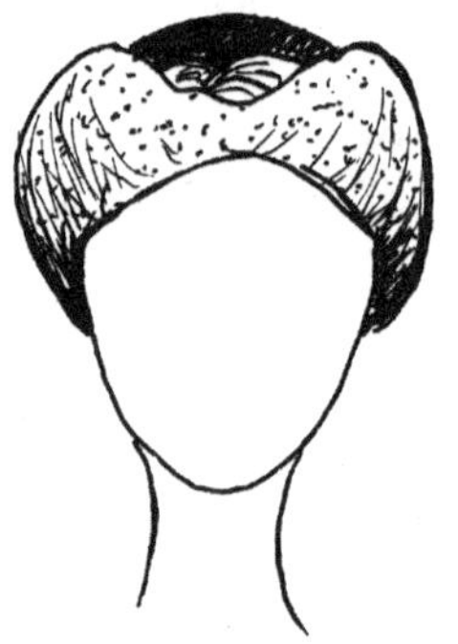

A scarf can be used as an overwrap, smoothing the look of the turban wrap. Lay your scarf over your turban base and tie your turban as shown in the top illustration. Next, pull the scarf up and around your turban, tucking to secure.

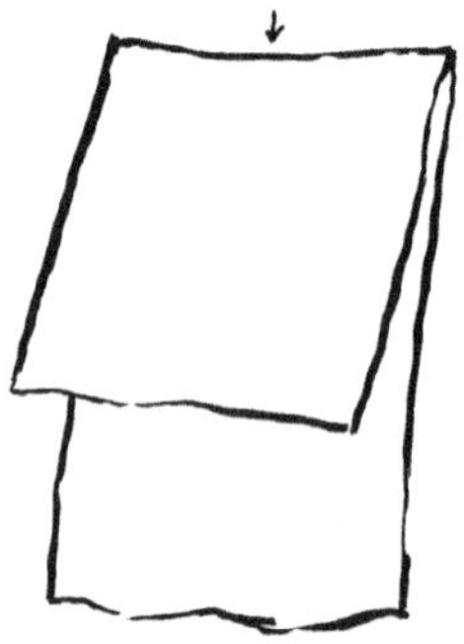

Veils

While many tribal dancers prefer to leave a veil dance out of their performances, the veil can be a very important costume piece. The veil can be used for many different purposes within the garment and be a versatile garment within the dancer's wardrobe. By wearing it draped off of the back of the turban, using it as a hip wrap or even performing with it, a selection of veils can add a great deal of color, texture and pattern to the ensemble.

Throughout the Middle East, women have worn a variety of scarves, shawls, and veils to maintain modesty and preserve their virtue. The act of dancing with a veil as a prop is a convention that was born here in the United States. Wearing veils is commonplace and socially necessary throughout the Near and Middle East. The dancer can have the look or provide an allusion to veiling by wearing a veil either alone or with their turban.

Veil with Turbans

The easiest way to incorporate a veil into the look is to wear the veil pinned or tucked into the top of the turban. Depending on the size and shape of the veil, this can create a number of different looks.

In the illustrations at bottom left, the dancer has taken her veil and pinned the center of one edge to the top of her turban. She has tucked the loose ends into the sides of her belt to keep them under control. This look will create a billowing frame for the entire body. The veil will billow and swirl during turns while remaining under control and behind the dancer throughout her performance.

To create this look, the dancer has folded her veil in half to start, then has pinned the center of the folded edge to the center of the turban. The two other edges are turned under. The tail that is created hangs loose from the turban down the back of the dancer, in much the same manner that hair would. When the performer spins, the tail will fly up, changing the shape of the body.

The veil can also be laid over the turban base before the turban is tied onto the head. This will create a long flowing line from below the level of the turban. This effect can mimic the look of long hair. Some dancers even layer a smaller veil over a larger one for a complex layered effect. It is still a good idea to wear a head cloth beneath the veil. It keeps the entire headdress from slipping and absorbs perspiration, helping to keep your veil clean.

The drawing at the top left shows a dancer with a short veil laid under her turban. This short veil can also be pulled up and wrapped around the turban, giving a smooth look to the turban, as also shown.

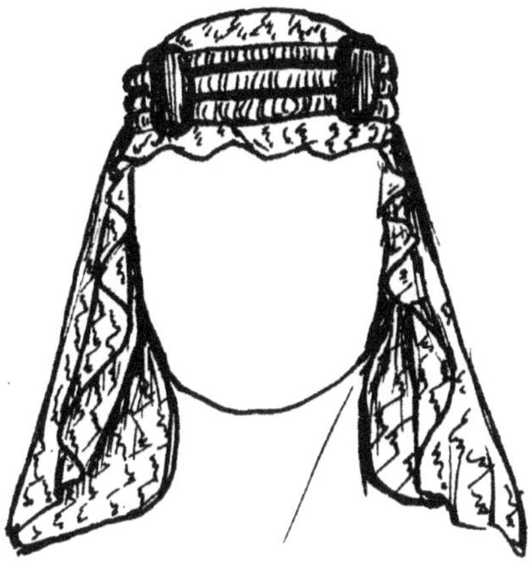

Kaffiyeh and agal

Using Ropes or Ties

The simplest form of veiling is to merely lay a veil across your head and tie it down with a cord or with a second twisted veil. This style resembles the traditional Arabian men's headgear, the kaffiyeh and agal. Variations on this style are easy to pull together and require less practice than tying a turban. Simply lay a folded square or rectangle with the fold centered over your forehead. Take the second scarf or veil and twist it into a rope. Wrap the rope around your head tying in the back. This rope can be composed of one or more scarves twisted together, or it can be wrapped with a string of beads, cording or even a simple length of ribbon (left, below).

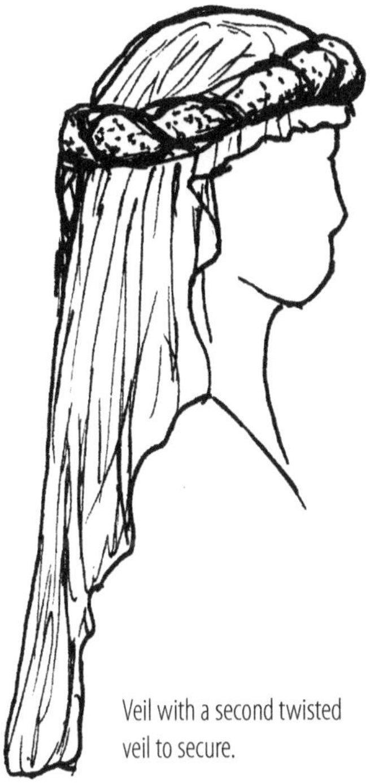

Veil with a second twisted veil to secure.

Even when wearing different styles of choli, the tribal style still maintains its unified look.

5 The Choli and Bra

The *choli* is a short bodice or blouse from India. It evolved from the simple breast wrap that was common throughout the Indian sub continent and as far east as Burma and Siam (now Thailand). With the spread of Islam across Asia during the 8th century, the need for a more substantial garment changed the native attire to fit the proscriptions of this new religion. The choli became the foundation upon which the *sari*, a length of uncut cloth, was wrapped. The sari is a very functional garment, as it can be turned into a rain cover, child carrier or sack with a simple twist and the tying of a knot.

In a hot and humid climate, the choli was an effective garment for keeping the bustline covered while allowing the arms, back and stomach regions to remain unclothed. The sari could be worn in any number of configurations. Even today, the manner in which the sari is wrapped and draped is socially coded and exhibit many regional variations.

Above and right: Outside and inside views of a Ribari-designed choli

Eventually skirts were added to the choli-sari ensemble. In some ethnic groups, the choli-skirt combination became the principle mode of dress, especially among nomadic, rural and gypsy peoples. In Western India and Pakistan, cholis are often heavily embroidered and encrusted with mirror pieces. These garments are highly prized among tribal dancers here in the West for their exotic beauty. The tribal style favored by many dancers is directly related to the clothing styles of the Banjara, Ribari, Lambani and other tribal groups from this region.

The first time the choli was associated with any form of tribal-style dancing in the United States was by the famous Ruth St. Denis in the first quarter of the 20th century. Her dances were based on Orientalist fantasies. Her movements drew on traditions originating from India, the Middle East, North Africa and even included postures pulled from ancient Egyptian painting. Her costumes were elaborate assemblages of elements from these far-flung regions. Her Nautch dance was performed wearing a choli-skirt ensemble wrapped with veil made of asyute fabric from Egypt.

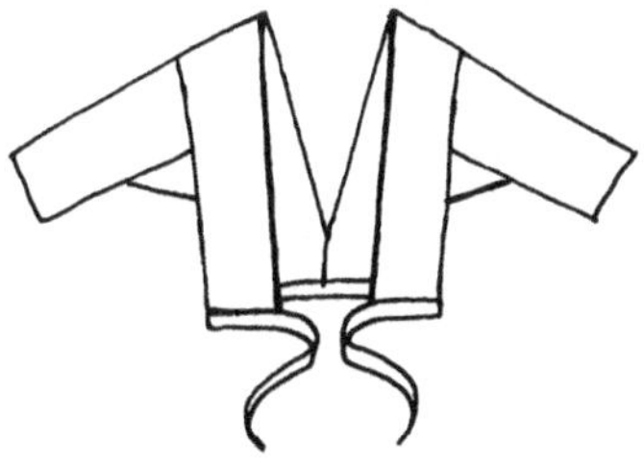

Traditional choli, front

The choli has been gaining in importance for belly dance attire since the mid-1980s. As a favored garment for wear during dance classes, stretch cholis made of velvet or cotton lycra blends have become a staple garment in the dancer's wardrobe. They are adaptable pieces that can be dressed up or down depending on the occasion. Several major vendors carry stretch cholis making them an easy-to-find and inexpensive costuming choice.

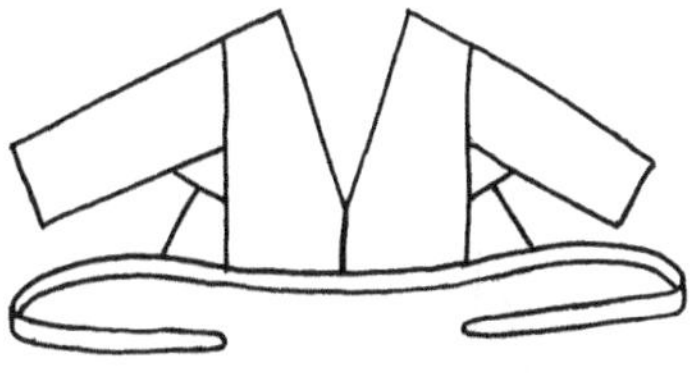

Traditional choli, back

Parts of the Choli

There are essentially only three major stylistic groups of cholis for tribal dance: the fitted choli, the stretch choli and imported originals from India. Fitted choli are made of woven fabrics that are designed to fit the breast region through the use of darts, gathers and seams. The stretch choli relies on the stretchy quality of a fabric, usually a cotton/Lycra blend or stretch velvet material to support the bosom. Other distinctive features of the choli include:

Backless construction that relies on ties to hold the garment closed. The most common configuration is a tie at the neck and around the chest band. Crisscross ties are one popular variation that appears on stretch cholis.

Sleeves. They can come in almost any length from full length to a tiny cap. They can be fitted or somewhat loose and frequently feature a gusset in the underarm region to allow for a full range of movement

Cholis are short garments that are fitted with a band under the bust line. In fitted woven choli, there are sometimes long aprons of fabric that hang as far as the hip region. The chest band creates tension to keep the choli firm against the body and supports the bustline.

Fitted Choli Styles

There are three styles of fitted choli that are easy to adapt from the standard fitted sloper. They require a series of measurements for the construction process.

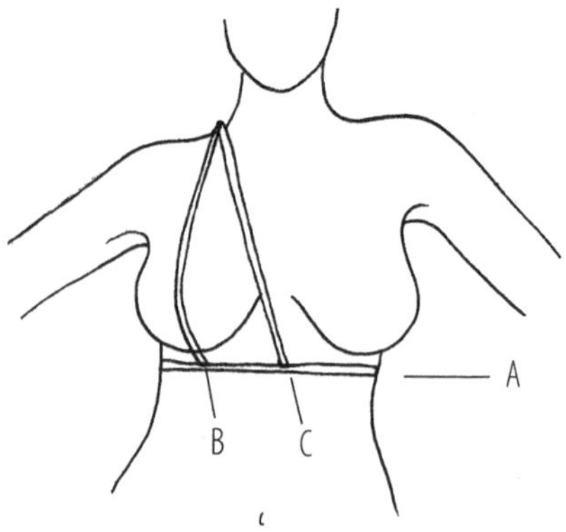

Step 1: Measure around the chest under the bust line (A). Make sure to measure in the location you want the choli to ride. A string or ribbon tied around the chest can make it easy to ensure that you are measuring along a horizontal line. Most women wear their choli band in the same location as their bra. However, you cannot go by your bra measurement to determine this measurement.

Step 2: Measure from the top of your shoulder across the fullest portion of your breast to the chest band level (B). This should be your longest measurement.

Step 3: Finally, measure from the top of your shoulder next to your neck down to the chest band at the center of your body (C). This line will help determine the shape of your cup. If you have large or very full breasts, you may want to repeat this process on the outside of your bust mound as well.

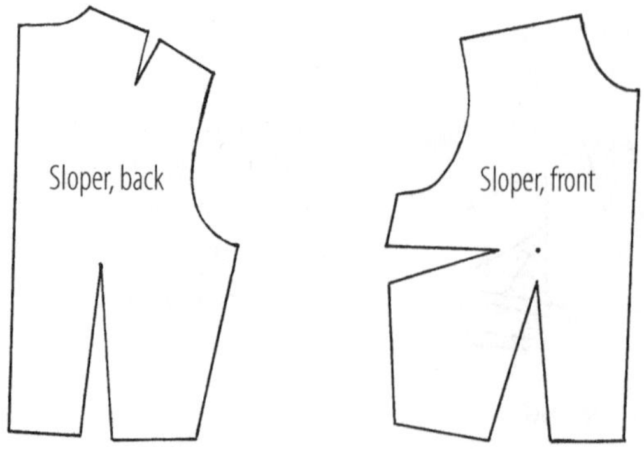

One-Dart Choli

This choli pattern is developed from the basic sloper described in Chapter Two. Before you begin this project, make sure that you fit the sloper to yourself and have transferred the marking to the pattern. The better that your sloper fits, the better the final results will be.

Step 1: Begin by converting the sloper from two darts to one. This technique is called combining the darts. Draw a line from the tips of both darts. The intersection point should be your bust point. Cut along this line until you are almost to, but not through, that point.

Step 2: Next, swing the lower corner of the pattern upwards until the side bust dart is closed. Line up the side seam and tape the pattern piece down. This has created a larger opening for the lower dart.

Step 3: Take a series of measurements. First, tie a string around your ribcage at the level you would like your chest band to ride. Next, measure from the side of your neck down over the fullest part of your bust to the string. Then measure from the same position next to your neck across your chest to the center at the string level. The side seam is straight across from the center point.

Step 4: Mark these lines on your pattern. This will mark the bottom edge of your choli. Transfer the mark from the center of the dart to the dart legs. Connect the center point to the center dart leg and the side point to the side dart leg. Remove the excess pattern below this line.

Step 5: This is your pattern for a one-dart choli. Draw in your neck line at the angle you prefer. Add seam allowances and stitch together using the sleeve pattern from the sloper cut to the length you desire.

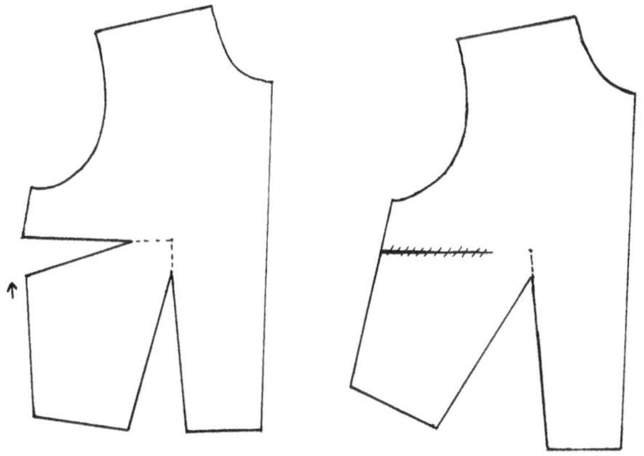

Steps 1 & 2: Combine the darts

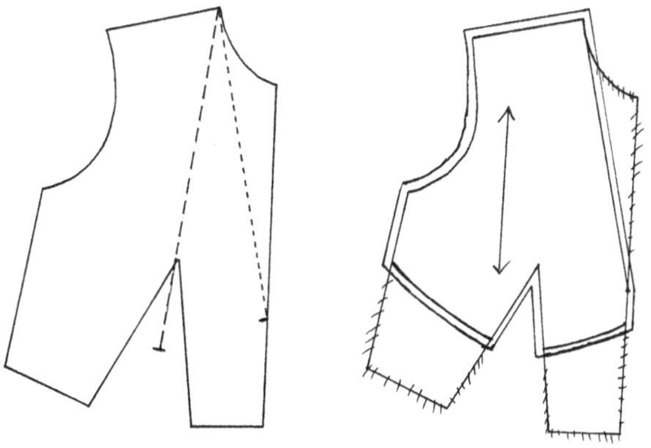

Step 4: Remove bottom of bodice

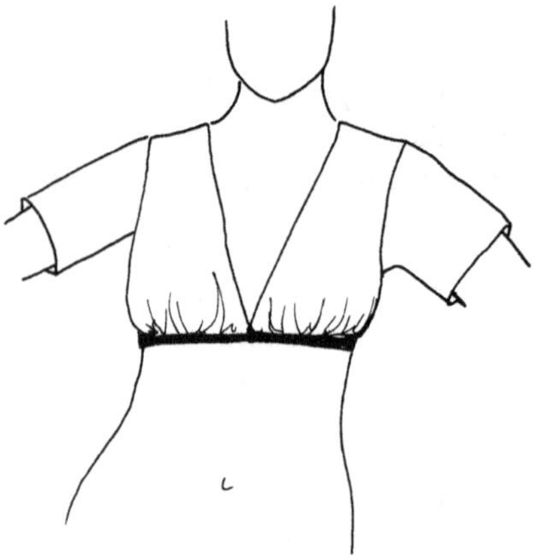

Gathered Choli

The gathered choli is a simple modification from the one dart choli. In this style, you round out the bottom edge of the choli and gather the area that would have been a dart in the other style. If you prefer to add more fullness, slide up from the center of the dart to, but not through, the shoulder line and widen an inch or two. This will create more gathers for a larger bust mound.

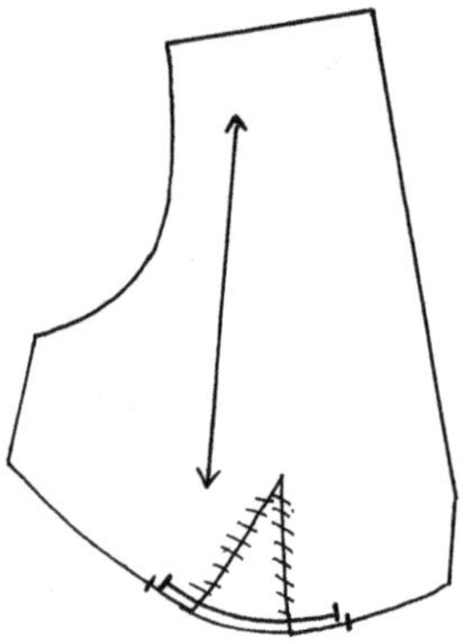

Princessline Choli

In this choli, a seam creates the shape. The benefit of the princess line is that you can get a very close fit for the choli. It is also a very flattering line that can be used to do color blocking.

Step 1: Starting with the one dart choli pattern, Draw a line from the tip of the dart up through the bust point and up towards the shoulder. Mark a short line across your new line at two points. One at the top of the dart and another some where between the bust point and the shoulder line.

Step 2: Cut along the line and separate the two pieces. Add seam allowances and stitch up a sample. Fit the sample to your body, making adjustments to enlarge or diminish the amount of shaping.

Step 3: To adjust the line, put the sample choli on inside out. Make adjustments on the exposed seam.

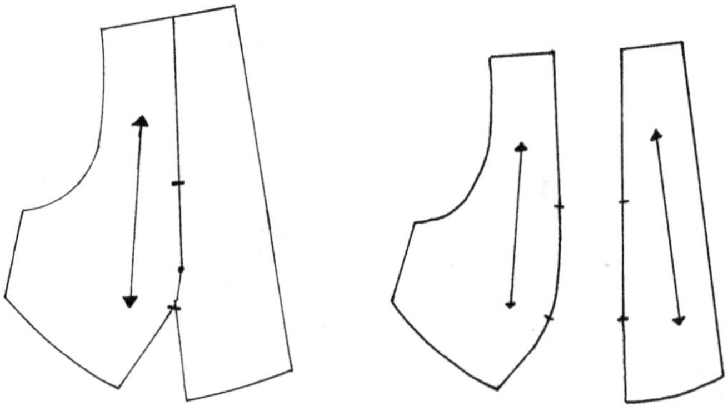

Choli Hints and Tips

Making fitted choli can take patience and thought, however, the results can be fulfilling. Make sure you save your pattern so that you can make whole wardrobe of cholis for yourself. Here are some things to keep in mind when developing your patterns.

- If the neckline sags, try taking a pinch of fabric at the shoulder line and re adjusting from the top.
- Make sure that all of your cholis have a strong chest band. A good rule of thumb is to make the band 15 inches (40 cm) longer on each end than you need to create your ties. You can cut them down if you need to, but adding choli ties can be a frustrating and the results can be ugly. Rule of thumb: the choli band should be the ribcage measurement plus 30", or 75 cm, (that's 15" on each side).
- If you have difficulty tying a choli behind you, extend the ties to wrap around the front of the body to tie or hook in the front. Make your band twice as long as your chest measurement plus 30" for ties. If you don't like tying you can fit your band to your chest and apply a pair of sturdy hooks and eyes to it.
- If you want a more traditional sleeve, you can use a rectangular shaped sleeve pattern with a gusset. To transform your pattern, simply draw a straight line from the bottom of your armhole to the shoulder. The sleeves should be the desired length by your biceps plus an inch or two (2–5 cm) for ease.
- To adjust the back, merely mark your side seam (taking the measurement from the front and draw a line across the back. Then draw a line from the neckline down to connect to that line. Cut away the center and the bottom portion.
- A pair of strings or cords is required to maintain structural integrity across the top of the back. Pin a pair of strings into place and try the choli on. You may need to experiment to find the ideal location for their placement.
- For the most authentic cut and styling, add a gusset to your pattern. Not only will this look great, but it will also provide you with more range of movement. The standard gusset is a diamond or a football shape that is 3 inches tall by 5 inches (7–10 cm) wide. You may need to adjust this up or down to suit your needs.

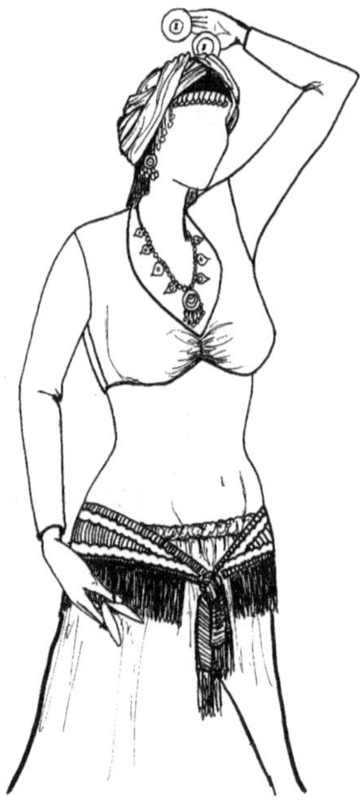

The Stretch Choli

The stretch choli is the chameleon costume of the tribal ensemble and can be worn for both performance and practice. Dress it up with ornate jewelry or wear it plainly for an elegant line. They can be made with long sleeves, 3/4-length or short sleeves. When you are making this style of choli for yourself, you can customize it for your needs.

The fabric is the key to making a stretch choli. It should contain Lycra or Spandex to give enough elasticity and stretch to the finished garment. While stretch velvet is a popular choice, cotton/Lycra or even a wild bathing suit fabric will create a distinctive garment.

Developing a pattern for a choli requires a different type of sloper. Beginning with a standard sloper will produce a garment that sags and hangs. This is not the look you want to achieve. So, the easiest way to make a stretch choli is to begin with a pattern for a long sleeved leotard. Most pattern making companies have one or two of these each year. They may appear in the costume portion of the catalog, with lingerie or sportswear. There are a few specialty pattern companies that cater to sports teams and make leotard patterns.

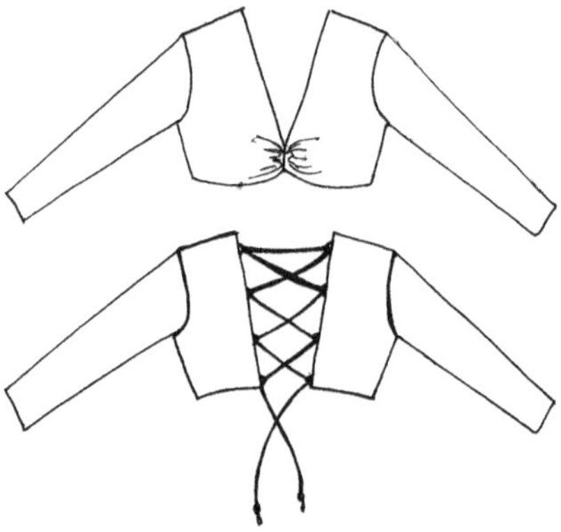

Above: Stretch choli front and back.

Adapting a Leotard Pattern

Step 1: Mark your measurements onto the pattern. Use the over-the-bust measurement and the across-the-chest measurement.

Step 2: Draw a line to connect these two marks and across to the side seam.

Step 3: Create your new neckline.

Step 4: Mark on the back side the same length as your side seam from the front.

Step 5: Draw a line from side seam to back and remove the bottom excess.

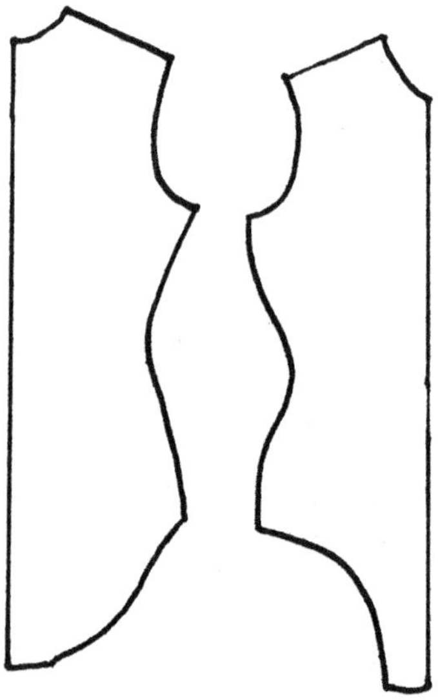

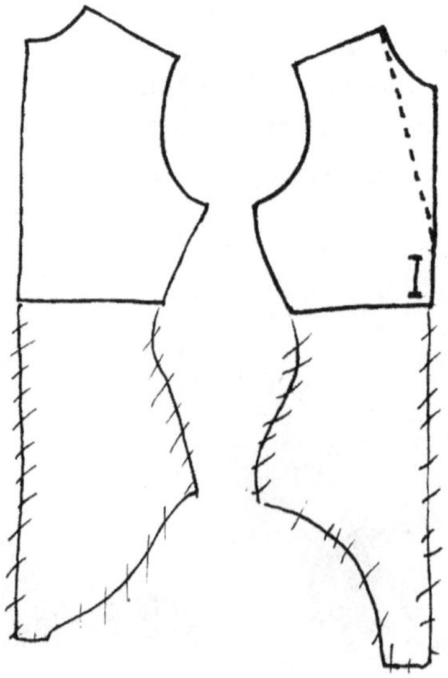

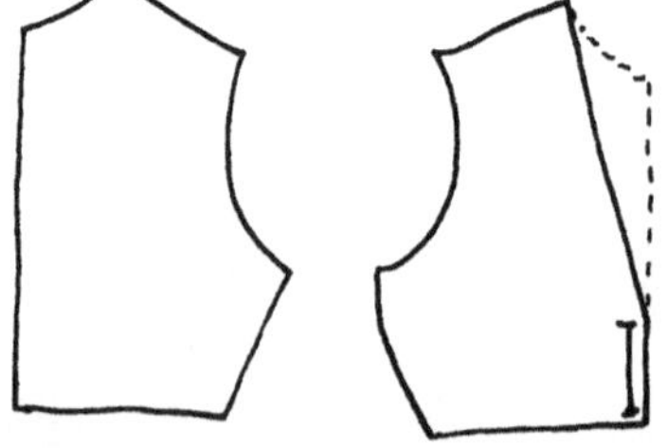

Far left: Leotard pattern.
Left: Adapting the pattern.
Above: Resulting choli pattern.

Adapting a Laced Choli Back

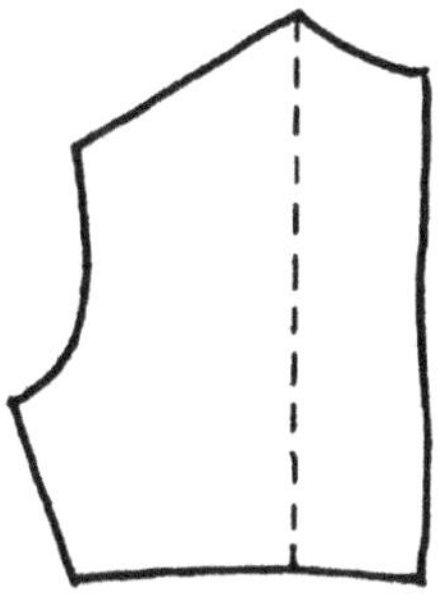

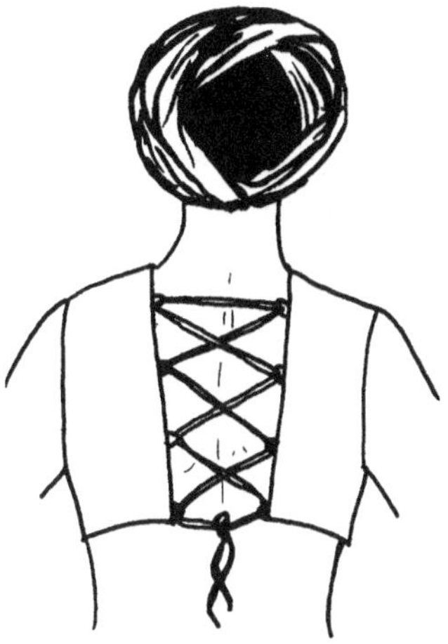

Above: The stretch choli needs more support across the back. Construct your ties and loops from a narrow tube made from the same fabric as your choli.

Step 1: Remove a central panel from the back. Draw downwards in a straight line from the edge of the neck to the hem.

Step 2: Mark the placement of the loops. You will need a series of three, four or five pairs of loops to hold the garment together in the back to maintain tension around the body.

Using a serger is, without a doubt, the best way to stitch a stretch choli. The process of serging creates a seam that is fully covered and will stretch without breaking. Some standard sewing machines come with a stretch stitch, which should be your second choice. Lastly, if you have neither of these resources, use a narrow width zigzag stitch with a short stitch length.

If you find that the bottom edge of the stretch choli either wants to roll up or is not holding against the body as tightly as you would like, you can stitch in a length of narrow elastic around the choli. If you decide to do this, use elastic designed for this amount of stretch. Look for elastic that is designated for use with Lycra, often labeled as suitable for swimwear.

The Bra

For many dancers, the costume bra is synonymous with belly dance costuming. Bras can be effectively incorporated into the tribal look by using tribal jewelry parts and pieces as decorative elements.

The bra is a garment of Western origins and has been used as a staple in Middle Eastern costumes since the 1920s. Performers throughout the world now employ the bra in most costumes; from glamorous beladi dresses encrusted with sequins with a hidden built in bra to the standard two part bra and belt combination that features lengths of glittering beaded fringe.

Below: The decorated bra is a very individual creation due to the one of a kind nature of many jewelry pieces.

For the tribal dancer, the bra is worn with another garment. It can be effectively worn over a stretch choli or with a scooped neckline gawazee coat. The bra itself deviates little from the standard lingerie style bra. The tribal dancer chooses a more modest approach to designing the bra, focussing on the jewelry over the top, rather than on construction techniques and padding to reshape and maximize cleavage.

Most tribal bras are built from a black base. The easiest way to make a tribal bra is to simply purchase a bra in black or a dark color. From there, the transformation is simple. Merely stitch on the layers of tribal jewelry, coins, shells, and mirrors that give the tribal bra its distinctive look.

Purchasing the Bra

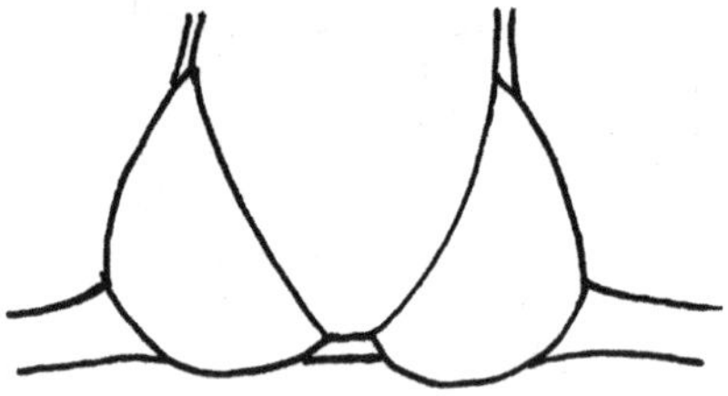

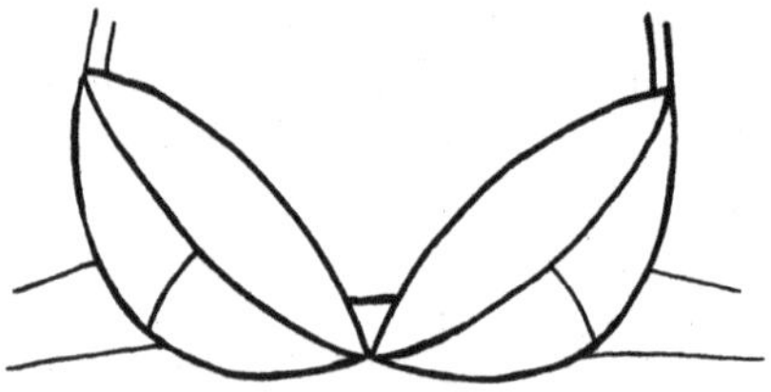

Look for bras that feature the following characteristics:

- It should fit comfortably. Try a few moves. Make sure that the bra stays put and controls the movement of the bustline.
- The cups should be made from sturdy, stable, non-stretching fabric.
- The bra should have good cup coverage that cradles and supports your entire bust mound.
- If you plan on leaving the original straps on the bra, make sure they are sturdy and wide enough to support not only the bust, but the decorations as well.

There are two major styles of bras that are suitable for transforming into a tribal belly dance bra. The first is the standard form-fitted bra that is cut in numerous pattern pieces to fit the bust line. No matter if your style of choice is a wonder, a miracle or simply fabulous, there are many different companies making these bras at nearly every price point. Another style that is widely available is the molded cup bra. These bras are made of layers of foam that has been molded into shape. Although they generally do not produce cleavage, these bras can form a solid and durable base for stitching on tribal jewelry pieces.

Transforming the Bra

If you find a fabulous bra that does not happen to come in a dark color, you can transform it into the perfect base with some hand sewing. This process involves disassembling the bra, covering the cups and then making new straps that match the cup color.

Covering Bra Cups

Step 1: Cut two pieces of the covering fabric approximately 2–3 inches (5–8 cm) larger than the cups. When in doubt, err to a larger sized rectangle; you can always cut excess fabric, but it's nearly impossible to add and you will have to start over if you run out.

Step 2: Beginning at one corner, gently fold the fabric over the top of the cup, pinning as you work your way across.

Step 3: When you reach the corner, make sure to fold the fabric neatly to reduce bulk (this is especially important when using a thick fabric such as a brocade or a velvet) Continue working your way along the bottom edge of the cup.

Step 4: Pause when you reach the center of the cup.

Step 5: Begin pinning from the original starting point down the underside of the cup until you reach the center.

Step 6: You will find you have a large pleat of fabric. This will form your dart. Smooth the dart fold in either direction depending on your taste and the look you wish to achieve.

Step 7: Flip the cup over and trim to a uniform 1/4 to 3/4 inches (5–20 mm).

Step 8: Stitch down the edges of the fabric using a whip stitch on the inside of the bra cup. Use a slip stitch or a hem stitch to close the fold of the dart.

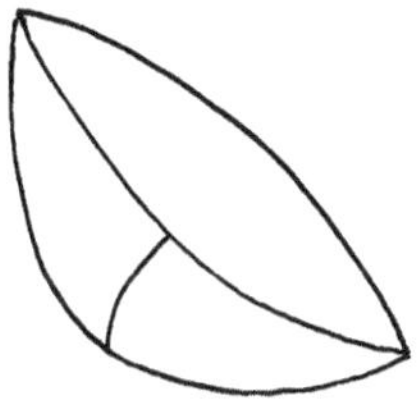

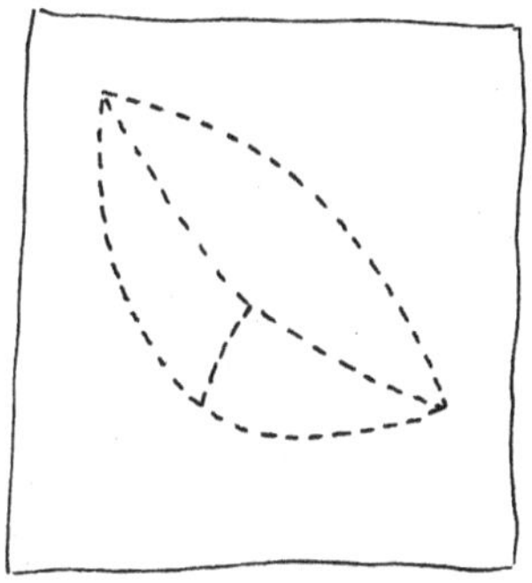

Step 1

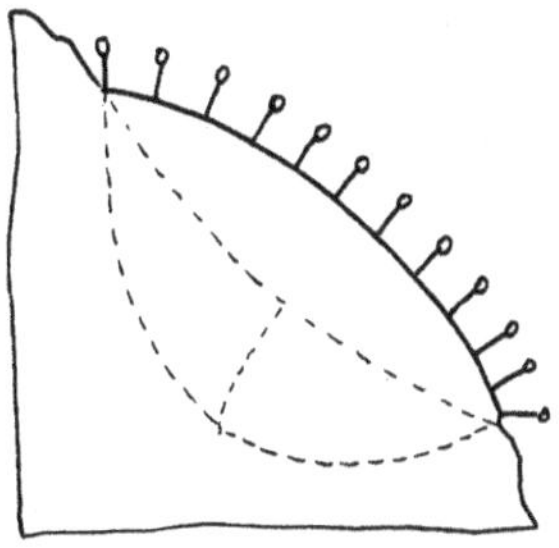

Steps 2 & 3

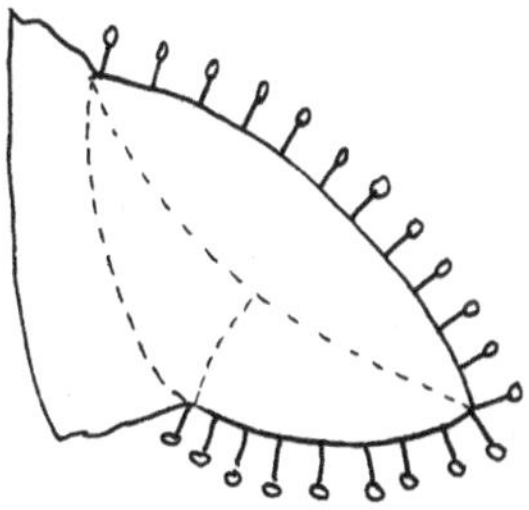

Steps 4 & 5

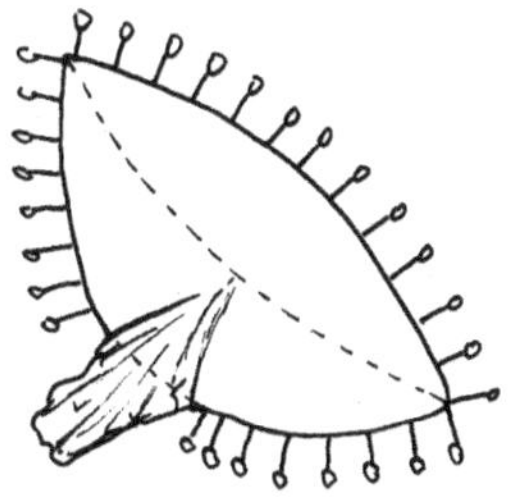

Step 6

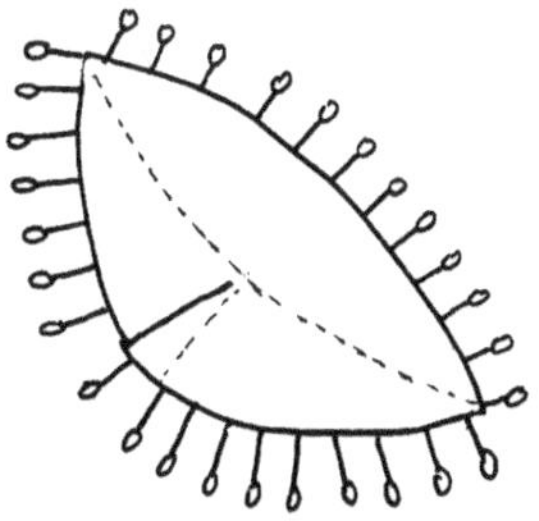

Step 7

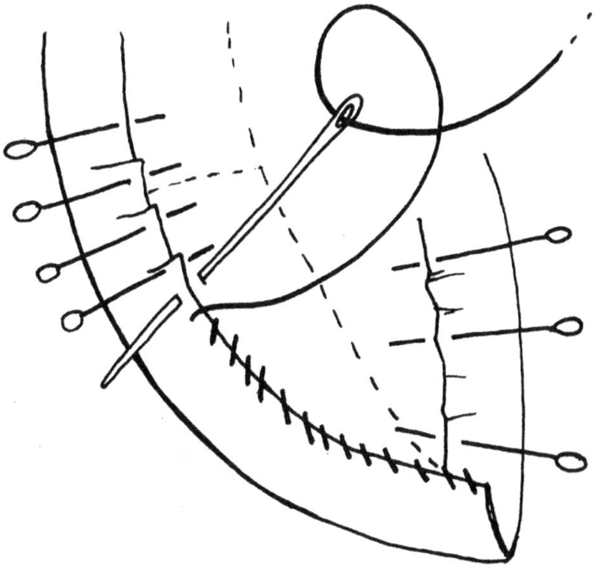

Step 8: Stitching down the fabric

Many dancers don't mind the straps of their bra showing if they blend into the costume.

The tribal bra looks good with gypsy costumes.

Straps

Once you have covered your bra cups, you will need to stitch them back into the configuration of a bra. Gros-grain is a sturdy and strong non-stretching ribbon that makes very secure straps. In general, the straps are left modest or unadorned; however, they should match the color of the bra cups. Attach the straps in the same locations as the originals, leaving a good length behind to put it on and adjust.

Unfortunately, there is no magic formula for calculating the lengths of straps. Generally, I start with a V shape of ribbon stitched to fit the width of the original chest band. From this, I extend a length of gros-grain that is longer than I need to wrap around the chest. I also stitch on the shoulder straps as well. Help from a friend will make this portion of fitting and adjusting go much easier.

To finish the chest band, making sure that they overlap. Fold under an inch (25 mm) and stitch through the layers to make a secure base for attaching the hooks and eyes. Once the chest band is complete, put the bra on and pull the shoulder straps over and pin into place. For more cleavage, pin the straps closer to the hooks in the back. However, you should position the straps in the most comfortable position for you.

Decorating the Bra

This is the fun part of the bra making process. There are as many ways and means of decorating a bra as there are different types of jewelry. This is all hand sewing, so make sure that you are using heavy-duty, good quality thread and strong needles. A thimble to protect your pushing finger and wax to keep the thread from knotting will make the process less frustrating.

- Stitch through the back side of the cup. This will firmly anchor your decorative items into place.
- When stitching items on in a row, make sure to knot between each object. That way, if the thread breaks, only one will fall, not all of them.
- Stitch dangling items from places where they will hang.
- If you are using a pre-made bra cover, make sure to stitch it firmly at the tops of the cups. This is the area that get the most stress and will also show the worst if the thread gives way.
- Inspect your jewelry pieces before you sew them on. Make sure not to stitch on any piece through a jump ring that has an opening. They can turn and slide off the stitches.
- Try not to use metal objects with rough edges. They can catch on thread and abrade them, casing them to break. If a coin has a rough hole, use a file to remove any surface burrs.

6 Hip Wraps

The final result is one of layered pieces building to a complex look.

A hip wrap or belt is found universally throughout the various styles of Middle Eastern dance attire. For the tribal dancer, the belt is transformed into a riot of color with glints of mirror, the sheen of metal and large bouncy tassels. This effect is created with many different layers of decorative ethnic textiles, coins and jewelry stitched onto a firm base, which is subsequently worn over a fabric hip wrap. There are an almost limitless number of ways to create a functional and opulent belt. This chapter will introduce the major stylistic features required to achieve the tribal look.

If you compare the standard cabaret-styled costume belt with the tribal belt, you will notice some features unique to the tribal style. Unlike glamorous, beaded, nightclub-styled costumes, the tribal belt is often wrapped around the hips and tied in the front and the long ties are left to dangle down the skirt. This makes the tribal belt a versatile piece that can be worn by dancers of different sizes and shapes comfortably. In addition, the total tribal belt is almost always composed of multiple layers of independent pieces or stitched together to create a unified whole.

Hip Wraps

The innermost layer is the hip wrap. The hip wrap forms the foundation upon which other layers are added to create the finished look. While a hip wrap is not an essential garment piece, it does serve several purposes.

Provides protection. The hip wrap can serve as a barrier layer between a metal or coin belt and an expensive garment below. An inexpensive hip wrap can protect the skirt or pants from excessive wear and tear.

Extends the wardrobe. While a dowry belt can be an expensive investment, the hip wrap can be inexpensive to make. A dancer can collect or make an assortment of hip wraps to change the look of a single belt. Through changes in color, texture and trim, a selection of hip wraps can totally change the look of even the most limited costume wardrobe.

Dress up or down. The hip wrap can be worn for performance or for classes. Some dancers even wear their hip wraps with street clothing for dinners and dancing while out on the town. Shawls can quickly become a hip accent when taking to the dance floor at the nearest club.

Coordinates the look. Troupes of dancers with tribal costumes can create a "related" piece with the addition of matching hip wraps worn under their dowry belts. This can be done in several ways:

- Same fabric, in same color and shape for a totally unified look.
- Same fabric, same shape but in different colors. Shows unification, but highlighting the different "identities" of the dancers.

- Same color and shape but made in a different fabric. Creates a unified look with subtle textural differences.
- Same fabric, same color, but in different shape will accent the individuality of the dancer while maintaining unity of color and texture.

Shawls, Scarves and Veils

Practically any triangular, square or rectangular piece of cloth can be transformed into a hip wrap with the addition of the knot. The only limitation is size. In general, you will need a square or rectangle whose diagonal is long enough to wrap around the hips and tie.

Shawls and Scarves

The nice thing about shawls is that they have multiple purposes and can be used in the dancer's wardrobe. Shawls frequently come with fringe already attached. There is a tremendous variety in materials available. From lace to cotton, from satin to velvet, shawls vary in style according to the season. When you are at your local department store, drop into the accessories department and check to see what is available. To wear, simply fold in half along the diagonal and tie in front or at the side on the hip.

In general, scarves are probably too short to wear alone. However, two scarves can be knotted on either hip and worn suspended at an angle down the front and back. Scarves generally don't have fringe attached, and if you are using a non-standard item, for example, a pair of linen napkins, fringe can easily be machine-stitched to create more movement. Don't forget to consider even the smallest scarf. You can use it as an appliqué or embellishment for a larger piece.

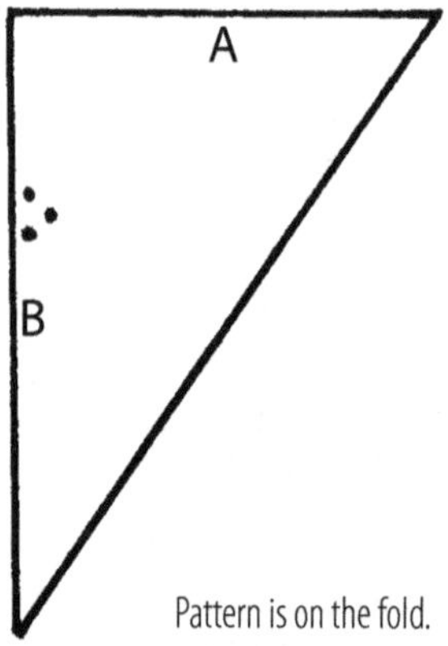

Pattern is on the fold.

Triangular Hip Wrap

Triangular hip wraps are, by far, the most common style of hip wrap worn under tribal belts. The triangular scarf adds length to the body and provides a visual break in the expanse of the skirt. They can be purchased from your favorite dance vendor, many of whom carry a large selection. However, a simple triangular hip wrap is an easy garment to make.

Step 1: Measure from one hip bone, around the back of your body to the opposite hip bone. Divide this measurement in half; this becomes line (A). Drop a tape measure down from your hip in back to find a pleasing length

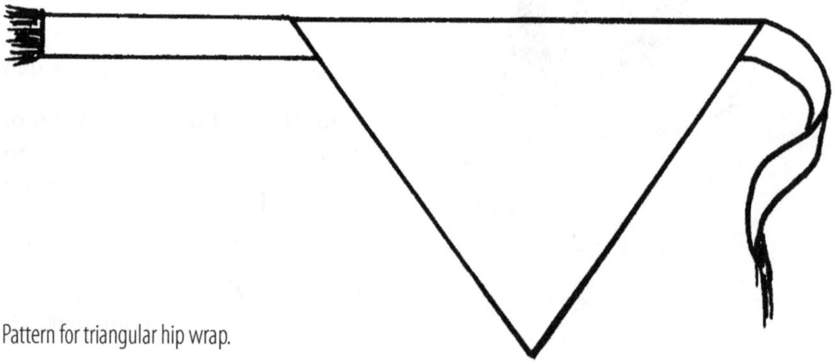

Pattern for triangular hip wrap.

for your hip wrap. Draw a line from the first line the length you want your triangle to be (B). Connect the ends of (A) and (B) to get the pattern for your hip wrap. Add seam allowances.

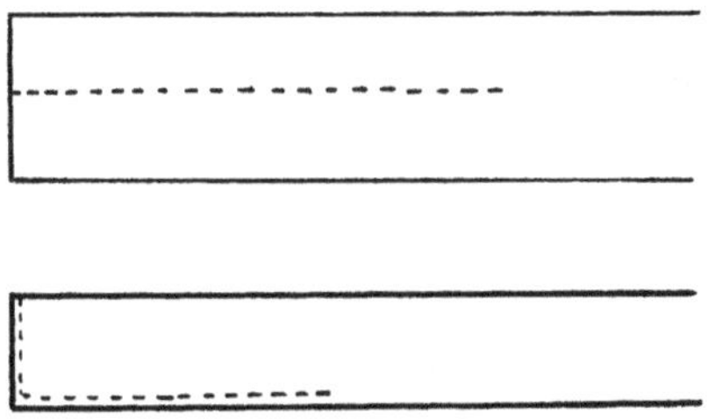

The pattern for ties can be as simple as a rectangle folded in half and stitched.

Step 2: There are two ways to construct ties. One is to use a single layer method, where the tie is hemmed on three edges and stitched to the hip wrap on one end. For this style, the general width of ties is about 3" (8 cm) high by about 15"–20" (40–50 cm) long, depending on the width of your hips and your height. The other method is to create a tube. In this case, the tie will be 6" high and folded over with right sides together and stitched. Turn the tie right side out and attach to the triangle.

Step 3: Once you have stitched the ties to the triangle and all sides have been hemmed, it's ready to wear or further embellish. Fringe is the most popular form of embellishment and will accent the movement of the body with their gentle flick and sway. Fringe comes in sizes from 1" (2 cm) to 24" (60 cm) and in a wide assortment of colors. Check your local fabric stores—especially upholstery stores—for the selection available to you.

There are other ways that the triangular hip wrap can be decorated. Be creative and inventive! Here are some ideas to get you started.

Appliqué. Even the most plain and simple cotton fabrics can be worked together using appliqué to create a distinctive and eye-catching hip wrap. Look to ethnic textiles as your source of inspiration for color combinations. A vivid red hip wrap with yellow and red squares or bands will transform into an exciting garment that gives the impression of an ethnic textile without the expense.

Textile fragments. Many dancers acquire parts and pieces of ethnic textiles. This is an opportunity to use them. Start with a base of firmly woven cotton, linen, hemp or ramie fabric. Cut out your hip wrap and lay it out. Play with the positioning of your textiles until you find a pleasing look. Hand stitch ethnic textiles that are heavily mirrored to your base. If you are planning on wearing a belt, avoid putting mirrored pieces at the top of the hip wrap.

Other textile ideas. Have a fancy embroidered pillow cover? You can use these by stitching them onto a hip wrap. Sari borders, imported braid and ribbon can all be applied to a hip wrap to give it that tribal look. Combine bright colors, pieces of different surface techniques together to form bright, colorful and exciting costume pieces.

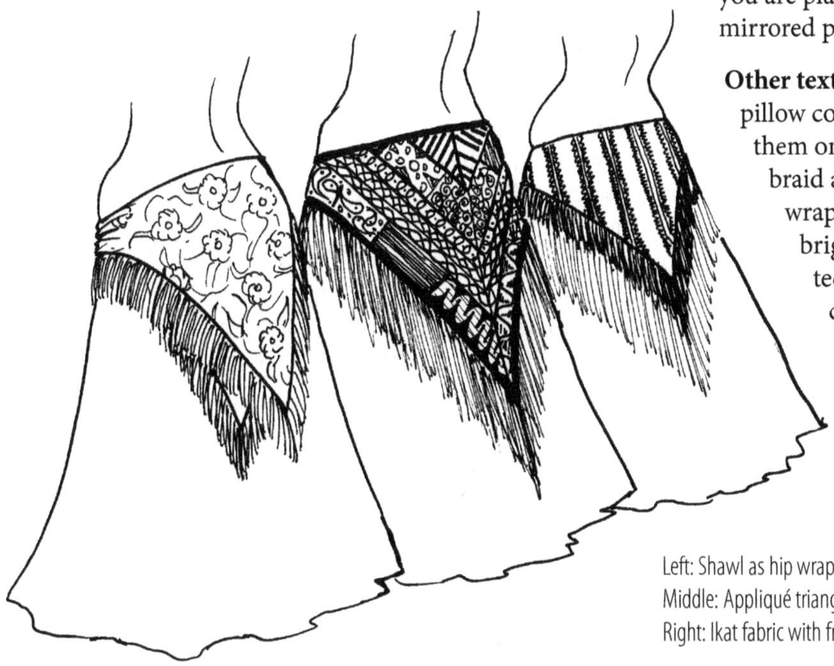

Left: Shawl as hip wrap
Middle: Appliqué triangular hip wrap
Right: Ikat fabric with fringe

About Belts

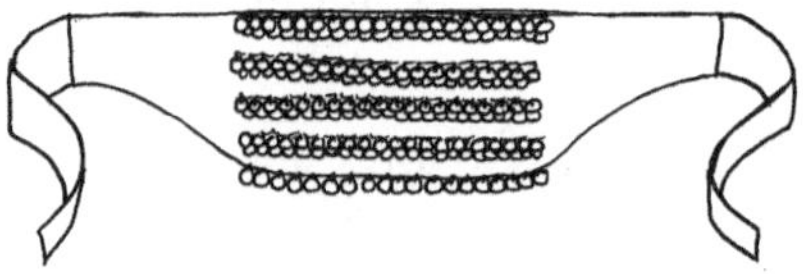

Many vendors sell hip wraps with coins and beads. Some tribal dancers use these hip wraps as starter costumes or as a way of unifying a group. These belts can vary in size, shape and amount of dangles attached. For the most "tribal-looking" belt, steer clear of any glass or plastic beads. Look for fabric bases that are in colors that fit your vision and color scheme for your costume. You cannot go wrong with red, black, yellow or orange. However, a lilac- or fuchsia-colored belt may not give the most "tribal" look. Remember, bright clear primary and secondary colors have traditionally been used in embroidery through the Middle East.

Coin Belts

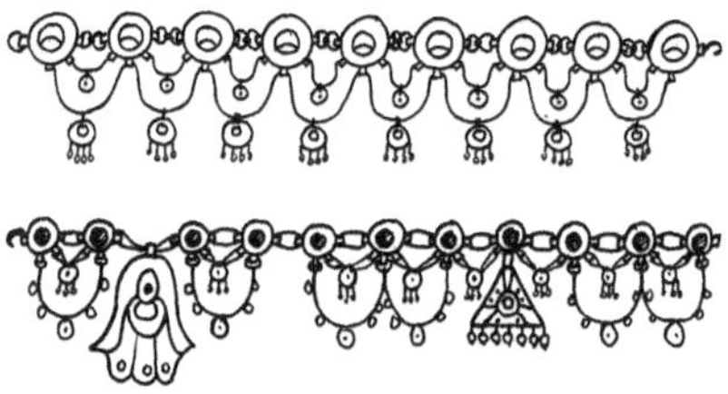

There are many ways of creating coin belts.

A good sturdy coin belt has been a staple of Middle Eastern costuming for many years. Coins have always played a big role in costume and adornment in the Middle East and dancers for years have worn coins on cabaret styled bra and belt ensembles. A metal belt constructed out of coins and jewelry pieces will provide the dancer with years of wear and is very versatile. While the dowry belt style is distinctively tribal, the coin belt can cross the boundaries from cabaret to gypsy through the various tribal styles and even into historical costuming.

These belts can be made by hand but require some specialized equipment and a good deal of strength. Using a metal punch, prepare your coins for mounting with jump rings and wire to chain. Tribal jewelry pieces can be incorporated into the design. Designs can be complex with multiple swags and layers of coins, or as simple as a single strand of chain dripping with coins.

A coin belt over a belt base with tassels and a hip wrap.

Inexpensive copies from India are available from a wide assortment of vendors. These belts are made from pressed metal rather than from authentic foreign coins and have a lighter, more bell-like jingle. The metal these belts are made with is quite soft and can pull, stretch and bend easily. Mounting them on a base will lengthen their life span by reducing stress from wear.

When purchasing either variety of coin belts, make sure to closely inspect them. All pieces and parts should be present and firmly affixed. The jump rings all should look sturdy and the chain should not show indications of metal stress. Fit is also critical. Coin belts are can be more difficult to resize and alter. Before you buy it, try it on. Not only will you be testing the fit and the look, but you should also consider the quality of its sound. Don't purchase a belt if you find the sound of the coins annoying. High quality coin belts with vintage foreign coins and jewelry parts may cost a lot of money upfront, but the investment will pay off in years of performance wear plus they maintain their value when resold.

Tassel Belt

Known as the tribal belt, dowry belt or tassel belt, this style of belt is one of the hallmarks of the tribal style. While other Middle Eastern costumes feature matched sets of bras and belts, the tribal style is composed of related parts that don't necessarily match. With this in mind, the tassel belt can be created using the materials you have available. While many tribal belts give a similar flavor or feel, almost no two are alike. This is due to the distinctive use of one-of-a-kind tribal textiles and jewelry pieces. Consequently, the materials selected for the belt will dictate the final look.

The belt is composed of three parts: the base, the surface design and the tassels. The construction of tassels is described in Appendix B. Many dancers construct a simple base in the shape of the rectangle. This is a very simple and effective shape. However, for dancers with a more curvaceous shape, a fitted belt base will stay put better.

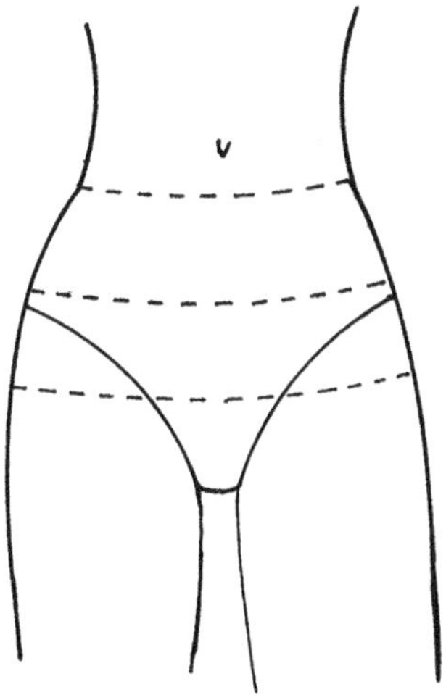

Before you begin either method, you will need to take some measurements.

Step 1: Measure your hip line where you want the *top* edge of your belt to lay. Also measure from one hip bone to the other, going around the fullest part of the hip at this same line.

Step 2: Measure your hip line where you want the *bottom* edge of your belt to lay.

Step 3: Measure the difference between the two. This measurement will become the width of your belt.

Rectangular Unfitted Base

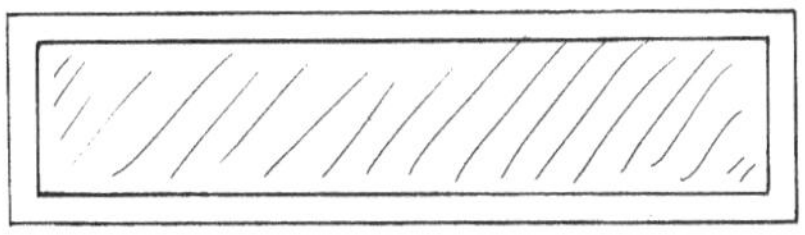

Position interlining centered on outside fabric.

This is the simplest belt base to make. This style is ideal for working with long shi-sha encrusted belt textiles. These pieces are available from vendors who cater to tribal dancers. Keep your eyes peeled, though; you never know when you might find a piece in an antique store, resale shop or import store.

If you are using a shi-sha belt, you may want to use the same measurements for your tassel belt. However, if you are using a narrow belt, or one that is short, you may want to make your belt base larger. This will expand the apparent size of the piece by forming a framework.

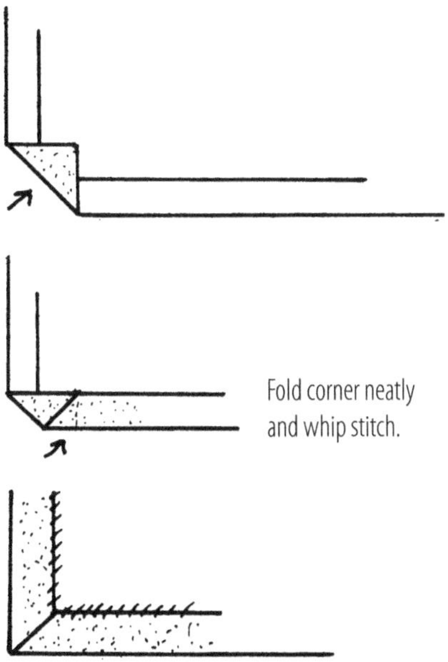

Fold corner neatly and whip stitch.

Step 1: Once you have established your measurements, cut a layer or two of strong, stable fabric. This interlining can be composed canvas, denim, heavyweight interfacing or felt. Many dancers have a preference for one of these fabrics or a combination. Experiment until you find what works for you. I like to use a layer of canvas and a heavy layer of felt. If you are using multiple layers, you may find that hand basting them makes the process go easier.

Step 2: Your cover fabric should be at least one inch bigger all the way around from the interlining. Lay the interlining centered on the cover fabric. Carefully fold the edges in and pin and sew. You can sew this by hand using a whip stitch. Or, if you don't mind machine stitching showing on the outside of the fabric, you can stitch around the perimeter.

Step 3: Flip the piece over and hand stitch any textile pieces, jewelry, shells or other surface embellishments into place.

Step 4: Attach your ties, making them long enough to wrap around your hips, knot and still allow a length to hang down the front of the skirt. This is a personal preference. To figure this out, you may test the length by attaching an inexpensive fabric strip to your belt and trying the look. Make adjustment and use it as a pattern for your final fabric.

Step 5: Cut a piece of fabric the same size as the cover fabric. Fold the edges under and press. Pin this onto the back side and stitch around the edges. You can use a whip stitch, a slip stitch or anything that is sturdy but easily removable for laundering. This hand work will only be seen by folks who are allowed to view the inside of your costume, so the technique is personal preference.

Step 6: Your tassels can be attached either before your lining is sewn in or after. If you like to change your tassels to create different looks, you may want to create loops out of Velcro or attach ties to hold your tassels in place. If your tassels are going to be a more permanent part of your belt, you may want to stitch them beneath your lining for a clean finished-looking garment inside and out.

The Fitted Base

The fitted base uses the same materials as the unfitted base. However, there is a little more work. This belt really only requires fitting across the bottom. For dancers with very round derrieres, this will make a more comfortable belt that will stay put. Occasionally, the rectangular models either slip down around the fullest part of the bottom or they slide up towards the lower back. There are two methods for creating a fitted belt; they will produce slightly different results.

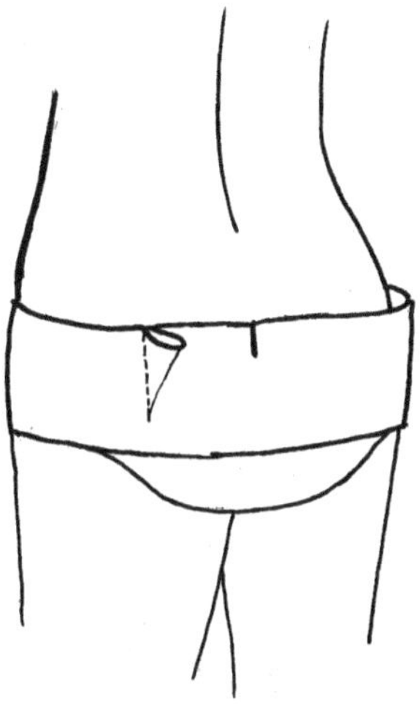

Keeping the center aligned, take a pinch of fabric. Draw a line down the edge along the dotted line.

Pinch method

This method is akin to draping and is easier to do if you have a friend to assist you. Extra hands will make adjusting the back simpler. To use this method, you will need a piece of woven cloth, such as muslin. Gingham is especially effective because you can use the built-in grid to lines to mark your darts.

Step 1: Make a rectangle approximately 12 inches (30 cm) high by the width of your bolt. Fold the piece in half and mark the position. This will become your center back.

Step 2: Line this mark up against the center back of your hip line. If you wear a body suit, you can pin the piece of fabric with a straight pin, Watch out! Don't pin yourself!

Step 3: Take a pinch of fabric about 2–5 inches (5–12 cm) to the left of your center line. Pin into place. You are making a dart that should be pointing straight down your body. Do the same to the right side.

Step 4: Draw in the top line of the belt.

Step 5: Draw the bottom line of the belt.

Step 6: Remove from your body and lay it down. Before you unpin the darts, mark the dart legs and the end of the dart.

From this point you can remove the darts by cutting through the bottom line to the bottom of the dart. Constructing a belt without darts will make the bottom edge a little looser. Otherwise, you can draw in your darts and use it as a pattern and stitch the dart into you final project.

Pattern making method

The other method for making a fitted belt is related to the technique of pattern making. You will use a sloper that you have already fitted to your body and transfer the markings to your pattern. You will need the back pattern to complete the following steps.

Step 1: Transfer your markings for the top level of your belt. You get this mark by measuring down from the waist to the top of your belt line.

Step 2: Transfer your markings for the bottom level of your belt.

Step 3: Remove the top and bottom of the pattern. You may wind up with three separate pieces or you may have one long piece.

Step 4: If you have three separate pieces, tape them together. This will cause the top line of the pattern to curve.

Step 5: If you have one piece, draw a line from the bottom of the dart and cut to, but not through, the end of the dart. Swing the dart leg closed. This will cause the bottom line to spread. Repeat on the other dart. Redraw your bottom line to smooth out these openings. Use the same construction technique as listed in the straight pattern, only you will be using a curved pattern.

Step 6: This makes a dartless pattern. If you want to construct it with the darts, skip the closing step and stitch the belt together with the darts in position. For stitching in darts, remove the area between the dart legs from your interlining materials. Close the dart legs and whip stitch the dart legs closed. Stitch the darts on the cover fabric on a machine as usual. Attach the cover fabric to the interlining using the same method.

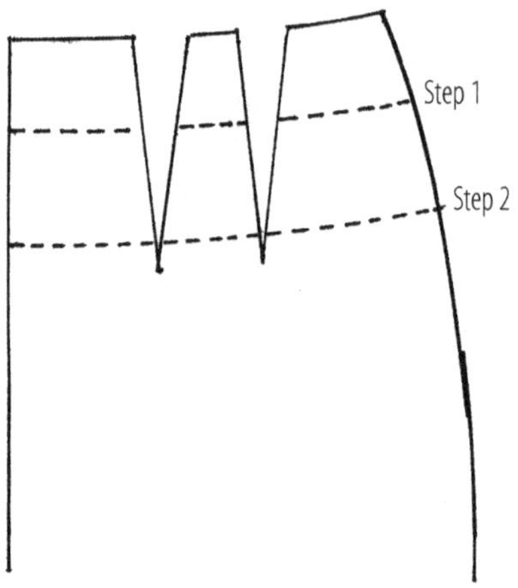

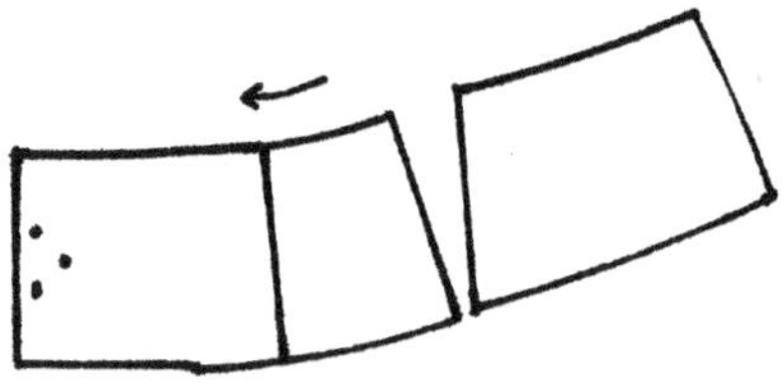

Step 4a

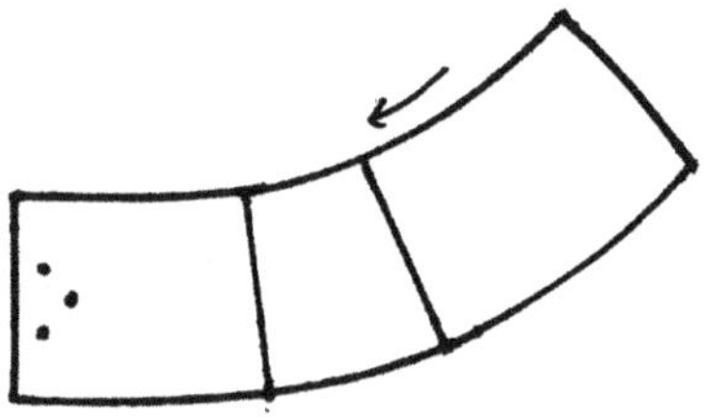

Step 4b

Step 5a

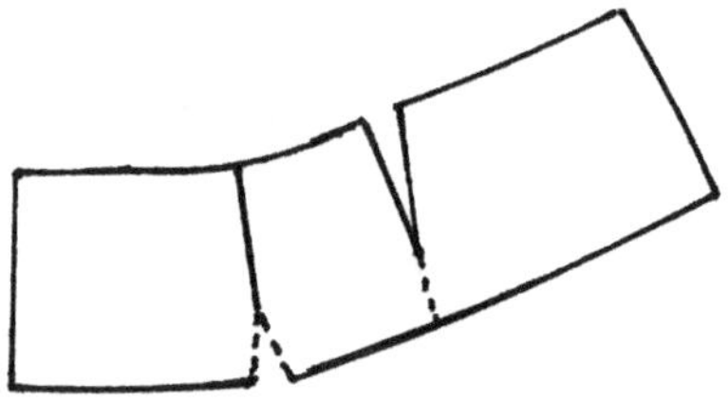

Step 5b

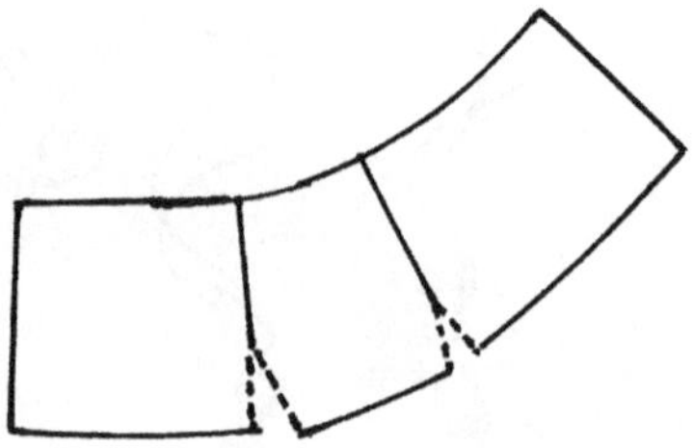

Step 5c

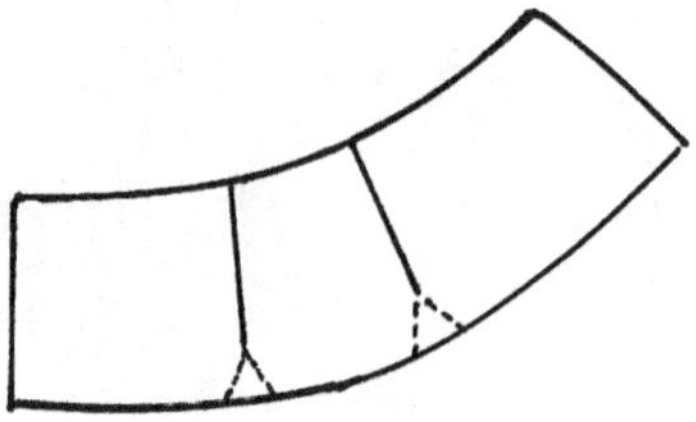

Step 5d

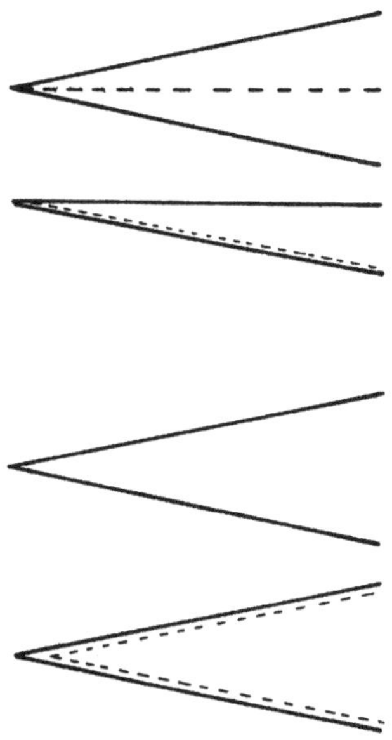

Top: Triangular ties made by folding a single triangle. Above: Triangle ties made by sewing two pairs of triangles together.

Decorative belt buckles reduce the bulk of a knot.

Ties

Once you have made your belt base and covered it, you will need to attach the ties. The length of ties is a very personal issue. Some dancers like to have ample ties because they like how they look as they spin. Other dancers like to reduce bulk in the front of the costume and use fairly short ties. The best way to determine the length that you like is to experiment. Use an inexpensive fabric and cut into practice strips. Pin them to your belt and tie around your hips. Cut the strip at the desired length.

Generally, ties are the same width as the belt. However, if your belt is quite wide, the tabs can be cut to taper. If you use a tapering style, you will want to either make a tie with a hem around the raw edges or cut four pieces. With four pieces, stitch two face-together on three sides and turn. Stitch the raw edge into the belt base under the lining. For a straight tie, you can save a step and cut one length double-wide. Fold this in half along the length and stitch on two sides. Turn right side out and attach to your belt.

Belt Buckles

Some dancers prefer to reduce bulk by attaching a belt buckle in the center front. Large two-sided buckles are available from jewelry dealers and in some specialty fabric stores. If you cannot find a buckle you like, you can have your belt ties hook in the front and hang a decorative piece of jewelry from the center front.

Other dancers like the ties but don't like the bulk of a knot in the front. A decorative pin to hold the belt together can achieve this look. However, do not rely on jewelry to hold a performance costume together. If you plan on holding your ties with a decorative pin, use a pair of large safety pins beneath to hold the costume snugly. When you can, use your jewelry as adornment rather than having it support the weight of your costume and the stress of your dance moves.

Tassel Placement

There are so many ways to organize your tassels. You can suspend them from the bottom edge directly through the top loop or you can hang them from long braided lengths of cord. You can suspend clusters of tassels from cords or have a single tassel on each. The options are countless; only you can decide. To get you started, I have included some illustrations with different styles of tassel arrangement.

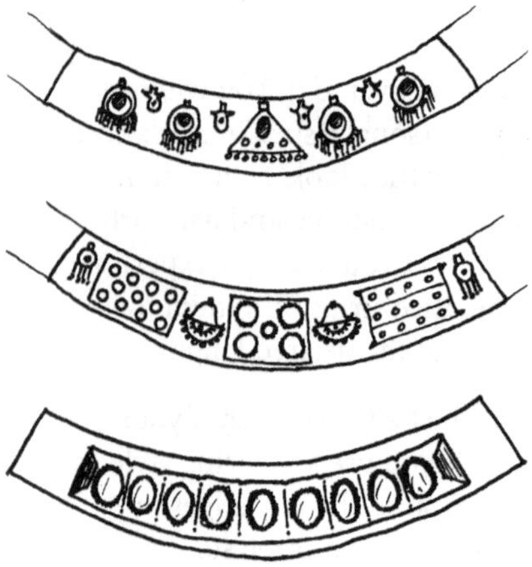

Top: Tribal jewelry belt.
Center: Jewelry and tribal pieces.
Bottom: Tribal piece adapted for fitted belt.
Below: Make your tribal textiles fit a shaped belt by taking small pleats along the top edge.

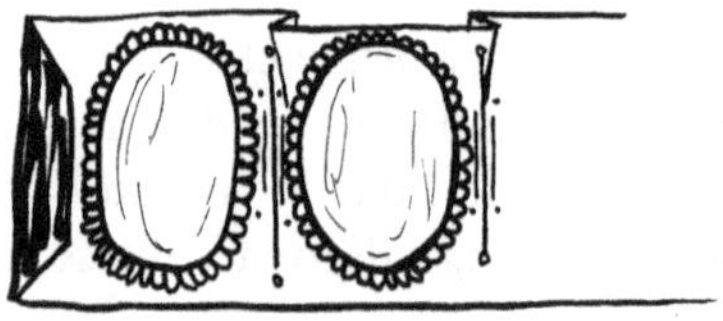

Hints and Tips

- You don't just have to use textiles on a dowry belt. The belt can be composed exclusively of jewelry.
- If you have several small pieces of tribal textiles, you can put them together on one belt even if they don't match. The goal is a look of opulence and abundance, not idealized matching.
- A toran can be an excellent textile for a belt. However, don't ever rely on traditional textiles to take the stresses of dancing without support. Attach the top edge to your belt base and leave the tabs suspended free to flip when you perform.
- The belt doesn't have to be rectangular. You can add triangular drops or even create your own toran-like tabs.
- Tassels and jewelry add weight. If you find your belt is riding up, you can try adding darts or you can suspend additional tassels, fringe or jewelry parts to help keep it in place.

Left: Tribal textiles on a unified belt base.
Center: Toran mounted on a belt base
Right: Tribal pieces on a shaped belt with tabs

7 Skirts and Pants

Skirts and pants can cross over to gypsy and other fusion dance styles.

The bottom half of the tribal costume is composed of either pants or a skirt and pant combination. The skirt is a costume piece that adds beautiful lift and flow to the costume. During spins, the skirt floats up gracefully, sculpting space and revealing the pants below. Pants can be worn without skirts under a torso covering garment such as a tunic or khaftan. You will almost never find a tribal costume worn without a pair of pants.

About Skirts

Skirts are an essential costuming element that completes the tribal look. Many dancers perform in costumes where pants are the focus of the costume, but nothing can provide the graceful lift and whirl of a skirt. The tribal skirt is generally quite full, long and undivided. There are two main stylistic groups that are worn with tribal costumes: the panel circular skirt and the tiered skirt.

In general, skirts are made from natural fibers, such as cotton and linen, but are occasionally made out of rayon or cotton blends. The fabric should be light- to middle-weight and can be just about any color that suits your wardrobe and the look of the troupe you're performing with. Because the skirt is a large expanse, it really has a profound effect on the costume. The color or pattern of the skirt can totally dominate the overall look of an ensemble.

Generally, skirts are made with either a drawstring or an elasticized waistband. Some dancers mount their skirts onto a yoke to reduce bulk over the hip region. The cut should be long enough for the hem to skim the tops of the feet when in dance position. So when calculating length, keep in mind the amount of knee bend you use when you are performing.

Measurements

Making skirts of either the tiered or panel variety requires only the most basic of measurements: the hip measurement and the length from hip to top of foot or floor. When you are designing your own skirt, you have a great deal of autonomy in determining the length of the garment. If you prefer to have your skirts hitting the floor, then take the measurements all the way to the ground. Many dancers prefer to have their skirts out from underfoot, and use a measurement from hip to the foot or ankle.

Tiered and panel skirts look good together.

Tiered skirts

The classic three-tiered performance skirt.

The most common and popular style is the three-tiered skirt. These are a fairly easy skirt to make and can be made as full as you desire. There are certain benefits of this style, including:

- The hem is on the grain. This means the hem will not stretch out over time.
- While three tiers is standard, you can use as many tiers as you like.
- The ratio of the gathers can really change the look of the skirt. Fullness can be added using greater gathering ratios.
- Several different fabrics can be used to create the tiers. Subtle blends of texture, pattern and color can give your costume a sumptuous quality.

Designing a tiered skirt is all about ratios.

Step 1: Take the hip-to-ankle or hip-to-floor measurement.

Step 2: Divide this measurement by the number of tiers you desire. This is the height of your tier.

Step 3: The easiest way to calculate the length of your tier is through the use of gather ratios, using the bolt width as your measurement.

Step 4: Calculate how many "bolts widths" will work for the top tier. Most fabric comes 44/45" wide, although you can also get 54/56" and 60" lengths as well. For most dancers, this will be one bolt width.

Step 5: If you use a gathering ration of 2:1, you will make the second layer two bolt widths. The third tier would then be twice the second tier or four bolt widths.

Step 6: You can mix your ratios as well. For example, make the second tier a 2:1 ratio, or two bolt widths, and then make the bottom tier even fuller with a 3:1 ratio, or three bolt widths.

To determine how much fabric you will need, add seam allowance to your tier height and then multiply it by the number of bolt widths you will need to make the skirt. So, for your standard 2:1 skirt, you will have seven panels. Multiply this number by your tier height for the length of fabric you will need to create the skirt.

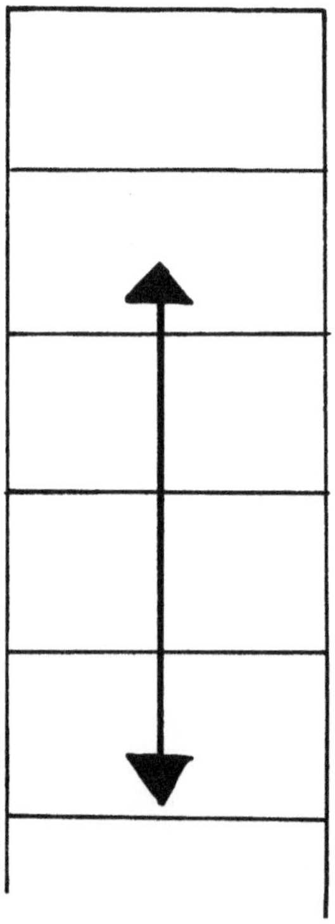

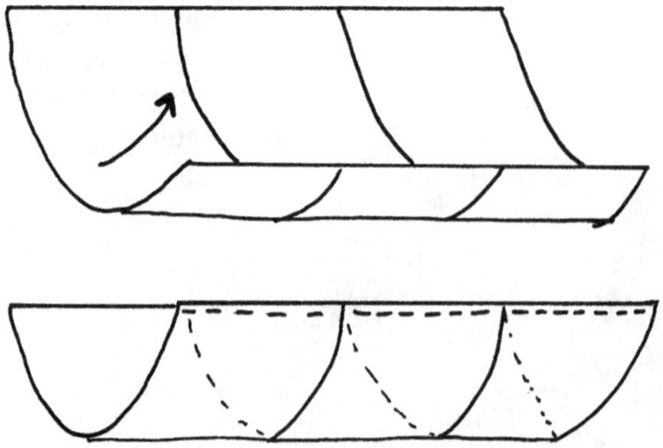

Fold your marked fabric lengthwise, adjusting your lines one over. Stitch and cut, creating one long tier.

Border Prints

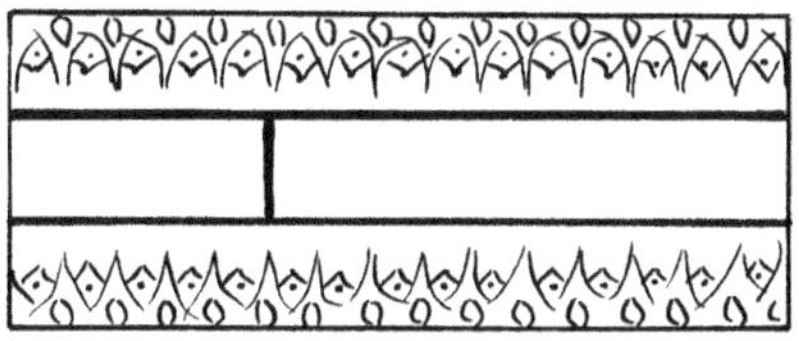

You may find a delightful border print that would look fabulous for one of your tiers. Calculate your skirt the same way as above. However, you would draw these lengths onto your fabric, orienting them in the best way possible for your boarder print. Remember, the height of each tier can be varied to accommodate your needs. For a woman who has a hip-to-floor measurement of 32" (80 cm), for instance, may want her top tier 10" (25 cm), her middle tier 10" and the lowest tier 12" (30 cm) to accommodate a 12" deep border. When calculating, you can arbitrarily use any of the "bolt width" numbers, or you can use a simple yard (36") or meter.

Construction Hints and Tips

Construction of a tired skirt can be quite time-consuming, but the actual technique is pretty straightforward. Below are a list of hints and tips for stitching up a great tiered skirt. Every seamstress has her own methods, so be sure to ask the designers and costume makers in your area for time-saving tips.

- Do all the vertical seams as one long seam. This will save hours of time when making a tiered skirt out of a standard bolt of fabric. On the wrong side of the fabric, using a yard stick or ruler, draw the cutting lines for your project. Cut the number of sections you need for the top tier. Cut the number of tiers you will need for your second tier and leave in a block. Fold your fabric lengthwise, but when doing so, shift your cutting lines over by one. Pin and stitch this into a tube. Make sure to back stitch on either side of each cutting line. Begin cutting your fabric in one long continuous strip. Do this for the second tier as well. And in a fraction of the time, you have one long continuous strip.
- Use a gathering foot if you have one available for your machine. Some sergers can also be set to automatically gather as they stitch.
- If you have to gather by hand, use the zigzag method to speed the process. Using a strong thread such as button and carpet thread or dental floss, sew a wide zigzag stitch over the thread to make a casing. Stitch the end of the thick thread down and pull the other end through the casing you made. This will cause the fabric to gather.

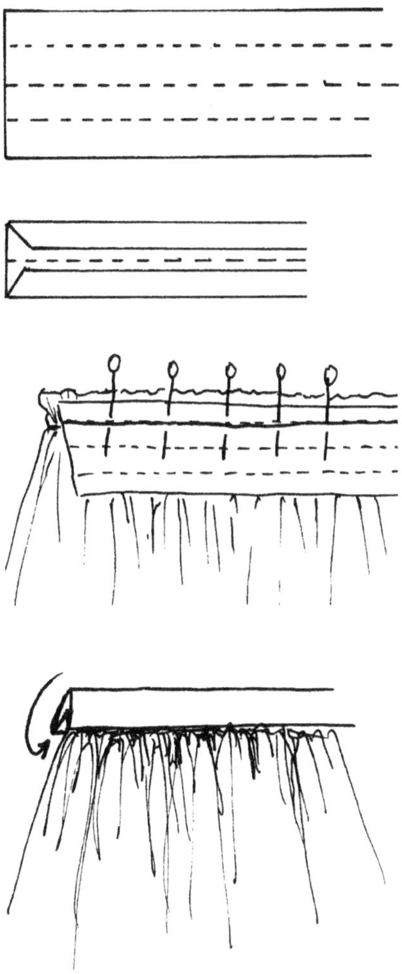

Making a waistband casing

First, mark your waist band. Double the width of the elastic plus seam allowance.
Next, press the seam allowances and the center fold.
Pin to the *right* side of your skirt and stitch.
Fold over to other side and either hand stitch, top stitch by machine, or stitch in the ditch invisibly.

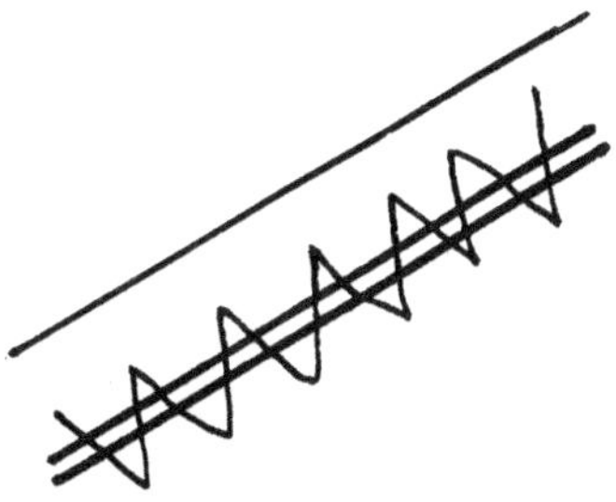

Zigzag stitch over a cord, thick thread or dental floss to speed up the gathering process.

Panel Skirt

Skirt with multiple panels.

The panel or circular skirt is made from a number of half circular panels which form a smooth, sleek, unbroken line down the body. These skirts have the benefit of few seams and reduced bulk around the hips. However, the most difficult issue for a full circle skirt is the hem. Skirts cut in half circles tend to pull on the bias. This can be avoided by cutting a circle skirt into more smaller panels, thereby reducing the amount of hem that is on the bias.

If you are planning on making this type of garment you should make a pattern. With a pattern, it is easy to replicate the look, make panel modifications and you can save fabric by tracing the pattern using the most economical layout. Again, this pattern is made using your hip to ankle, top of foot or floor measurement. Add approximately 4–6 inches (10–15 cm) to this length. Pin a string to the corner of your paper. Using the string like a large compass, draw a smooth curve. Make sure to hold the string taught for the most accurate curve. Add seam allowances to your pattern and you are set.

The circle skirt can come in several fullnesses. The most basic is a full circle, composed of two panels. A fuller skirt can be made with three panels, four or even as many as six! The individual panels can be divided to showcase a number of different fabrics.

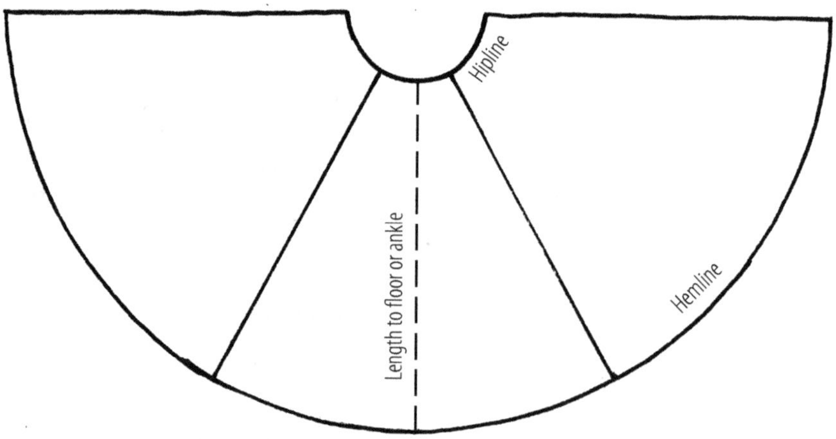

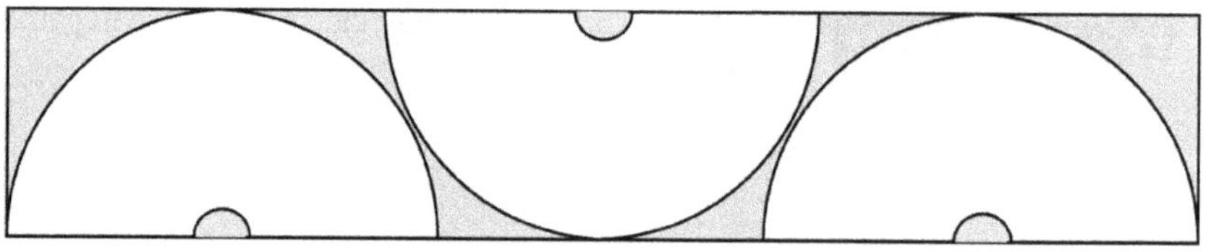

Layout for optimum fabric use.

The Hem

Before hemming a full circle skirt, let it hang from its waistband for several days to let the bias relax. Then, just before sewing the hem, trim the bottom of the skirt so it hangs evenly. The easiest method for hemming is to use a roll hem foot on your sewing machine. Otherwise, a simple rolled hem by hand will take care of the job.

Skirt mounted on a yoke.

Waistband

Because of the curve, the waistband cannot just be folded over to create a casing for a waistband. Instead, a separate piece must be installed to carry the elastic. This can be cut of the same fabric. For a one inch-wide (25 mm) waistband, you will need a piece that is at least three inches (75 mm) wide. A waistband that is four inches (10 cm) bigger than your hips will be easy to pull on and off. Some dancers make their waistband the same size as their hips and wiggle into their skirts or pull them on over the tops of their heads.

An alternative to reduce bulk is to mount the skirt onto a yoke. This yoke can be as simple as a rectangle of cloth wider than your hips and installed in a manner similar to the top tier of a tiered skirt. When you are calculating for a yoke, measure from the bottom edge to the floor. A quick tip is to buy a ready made pattern for a skirt or pants with a yoke in the size you need and use it to mount your skirt. This will save lots of time and aggravation in fitting.

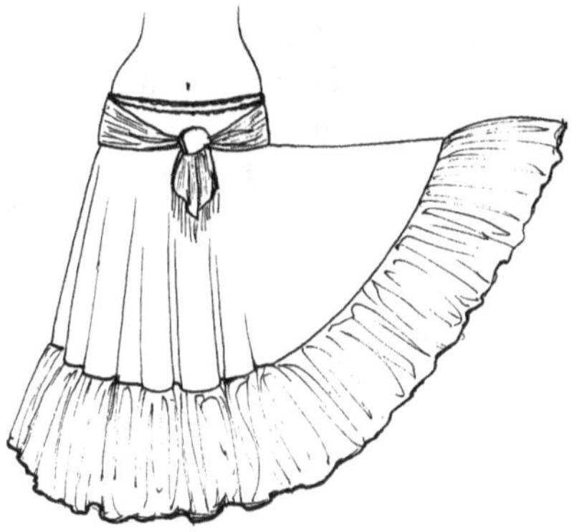

Circular skirt with flounce.

Stylistic Variations

Some dancers prefer a combination of styles. A circular skirt with a flounce at the bottom gives the look and impression of the tiered skirt when the dancer is standing still. When the performer spins, however, this type of skirt will spin differently than its tiered counterpart. This type of skirt can be a fun way to vary the cut and movement within your skirt wardrobe.

A single half circle panel can be a very attractive method of showing off a great pair of pants. For this type of skirt treatment, merely attach a single panel to a waistband, a set of ties or even pin it with large safety pins to the inside of the belt. This is a great use for a fabulous piece of fabric when you just don't have enough to make a full skirt.

Single panels can be any shape.

The same pattern can be expanded for fuller garments.

About Pants

Whether you call them *salwar, shalvar,* pantaloons or pants, coverings for the legs are essential for tribal wear. There are a few major styles of pants that are commonly worn with tribal costumes. However, there are many different variations on pants and ways of decorating them. From the addition of colorful panels of cloth, changes in fullness in the cloth and the use of cuffs to make a decorative field for the display of embroidery, there is no end to the ways that pants can be embellished.

Harem Pants

The simplest and easiest to construct style of pants is the standard harem pants. These can be developed from a drawstring pants pattern that you can purchase from any major pattern company. Patterns for sweat pants or sports pants are the easiest to adapt. Simply measure down from your hips, and cut the pattern down from the waistline. You may want to remove the side seam by laying the front and back pieces together and taping them down. Fuller pants can be designed by moving the two side seams apart and taping them down to long pieces of paper. The key is the shape of the crotch curve. If you convert or adapt an existing pattern, the crotch shape is already perfected for you.

Harem pants pattern

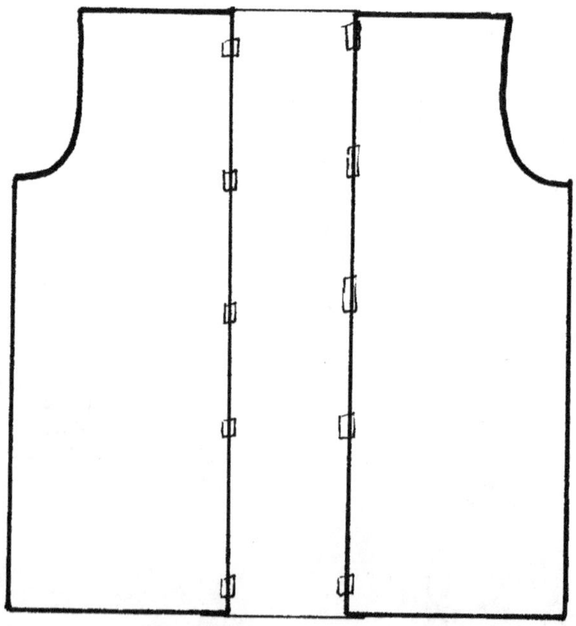

Fuller harem pants pattern

Indian Style

Popular in India and Pakistan, the traditional *salwar* shape is made from two pieces of cloth. Wide and very full at the waist, but narrow at the ankle, this style does not have a fitted crotch. Ease of movement is created by the volume of fabric through the hips and thighs.

Step 1: Measure from your hip to ankle (A). Draw a line down the outside of your pants.

Step 2: Measure your ankle (B). Divide the measurement in half and add two inches (5 cm). Draw your hem line.

Step 3: Determine how much fullness you would like. The width should be at least 10 inches (30 cm) wider than your hips. Divide this figure in half and draw a line at the hip (C).

Step 4: At the center front, draw the crotch line. To determine the appropriate depth, hold a measuring tape at your hip line and pull up and through between your legs. The most common length is at the knee, and can sometimes be lower. You do not want to raise this any higher than mid thigh. Divide this measurement in half and draw a line down the center front (D).

Step 5: Connect the bottom of the crotch line with the hem line in a long curving arc or in a straight line.

Step 6: Add seam allowances and an 1 1/2 inches (35 mm) at the top for a casing.

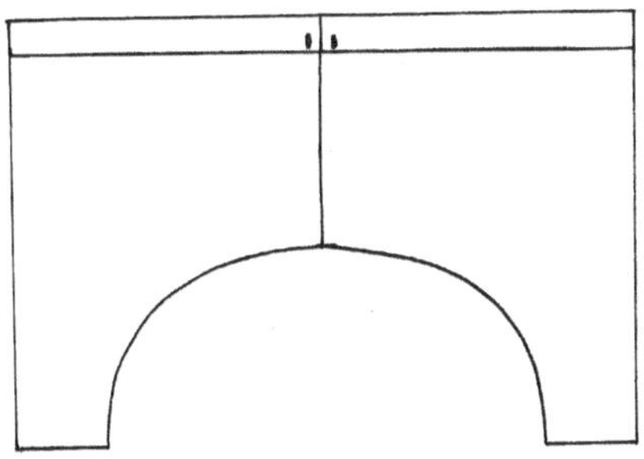

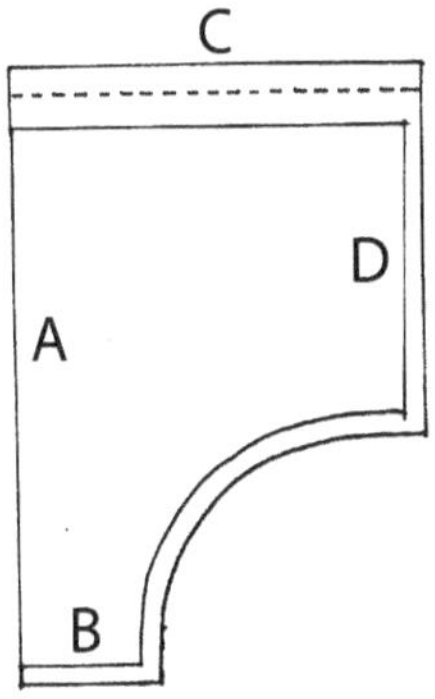

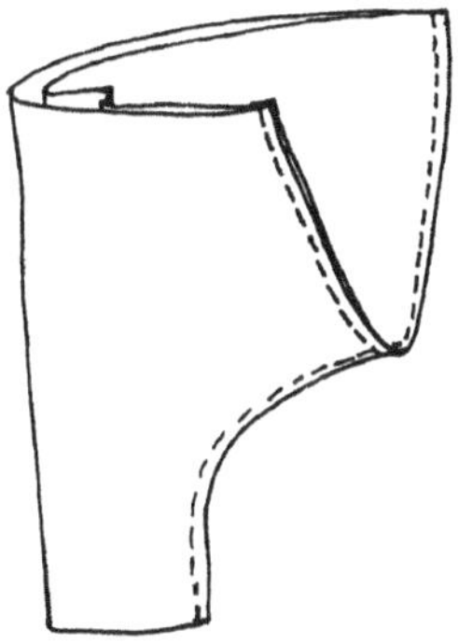

Making Salwar Pants

These are very much like ordinary pants.

- Sew in seam.
- Turn one pant leg right side out.
- Slip into inside-out leg (right side to right side).
- Pin and stitch along crotch.

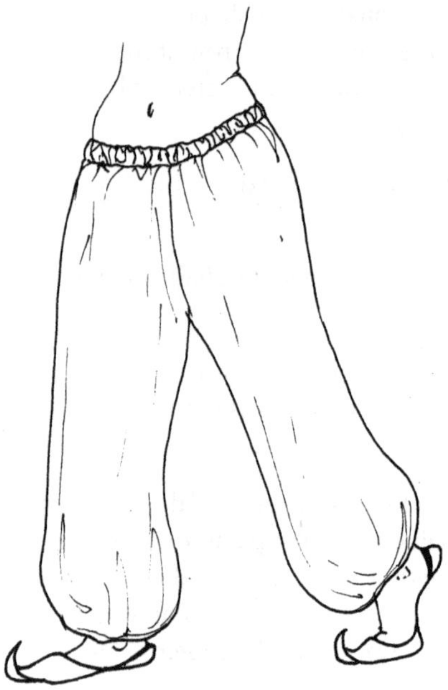

Arabian Style

Throughout the Middle East, the style that most closely resembles the harem pant is actually constructed without a crotch curve. This style of pant uses only rectangular pieces of fabric: a pair of large rectangles with a square crotch gusset that allows movement for the body. The rectangle should be as long as your hip to ankle measurement (plus a few inches for fullness) by the width desired for the fullness of the leg. The gusset can be as small as 7x7" (18x18 cm) although a square as large as 10x10" (25x25 cm) will allow more movement. If you sit cross-legged or perform floor work, you may want this to be as big as 12x12" (30x30 cm).

Step 1: Determine the level of your crotch by running a tape measure from hip level to hip level between your legs. Divide this measurement in half and add an inch (25 mm). Position the top of the gusset at this mark.

Step 2: Next, stitch the inside seam of the legs up to the bottom of the gusset and then along the other side to the top of the gusset.

Step 3: Perform the same steps with the other legs. Stitching the gusset to one side, and then stitching up the inseam to the top of the gusset.

Step 4: Stitch the center front and center back seams together.

Step 5: Stitch up the outer seams of the pants.

Step 6: Sew a casing and hem.

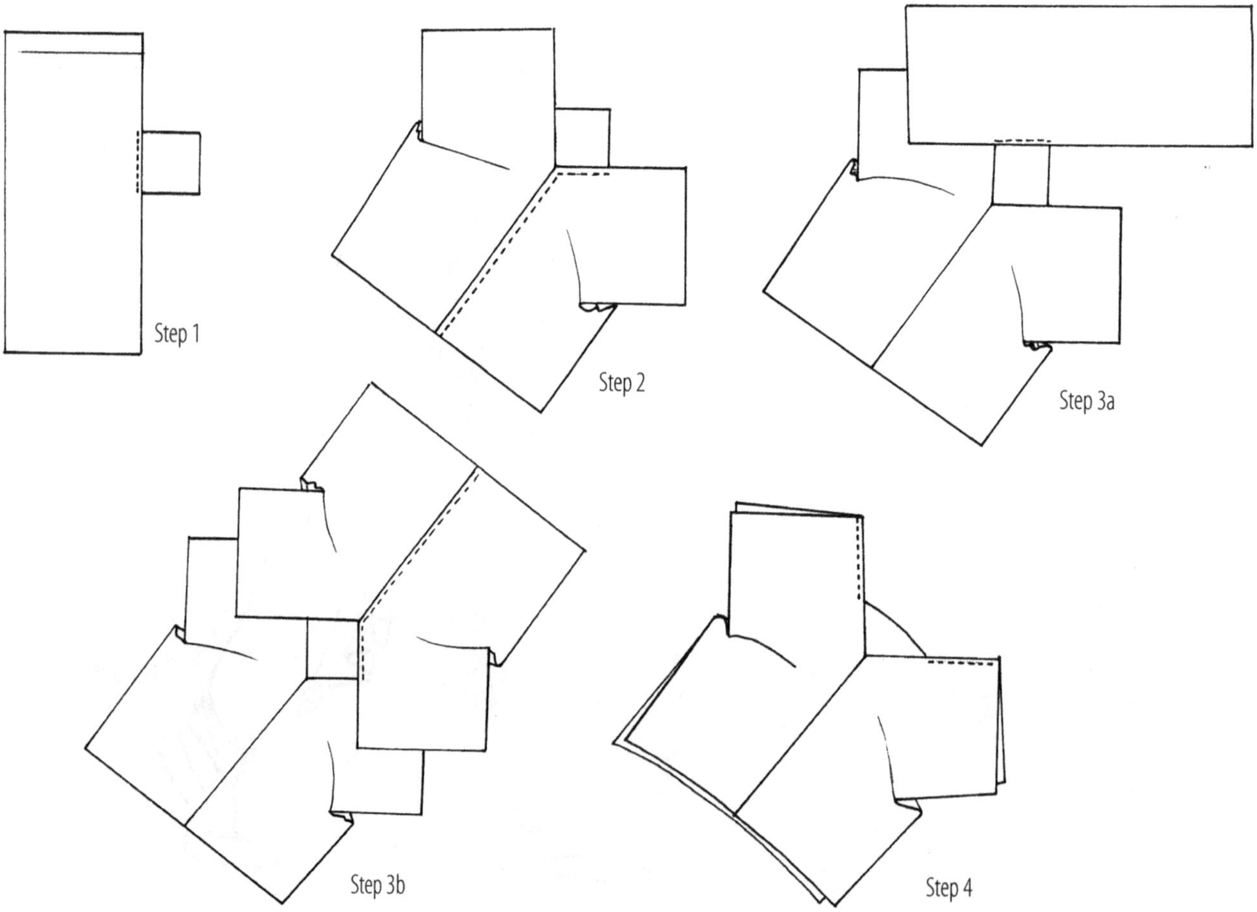

Turkish Style

Popular in the former Ottoman-ruled lands from Turkey across North Africa to Morocco are pants with a large rectangular gusset. These pants are quite roomy and comfortable to sit in. However, they have a good deal of bulk between the legs which can be awkward during floor work. Also beware: loose pants can cause chaffing in warm environments. Avoid chaffing by wearing tights. The style is composed of three rectangles. Two form the legs with a long central rectangle that forms the crotch.

Step 1: Begin with your out-seam measurement. Make sure to add enough at the top for a casing, generally an 1 1/2 inches (35 mm). (A)

Step 2: Next, determine how wide you want the legs. You may want to measure your calf and add 2 inches (5 cm) or more to this length. (B)

Step 3: The crotch gusset should be fairly wide. Generally, this panel is shoulder- or hip-width wide (the traditional width of a portable loom). Draw this line for the waist band. (C)

Step 4: Next, determine how far you want your gusset to drop. Drop your tape measure from your hip line down to the desired length and then up to your hip level in back. (D)

To construct these pants, simply stitch up the in seams to where the gusset will hit. Then stitch the large gusset into place along the crotch line. These pants, because of the volume of fabric, look especially nice when made out of extremely lightweight fabrics

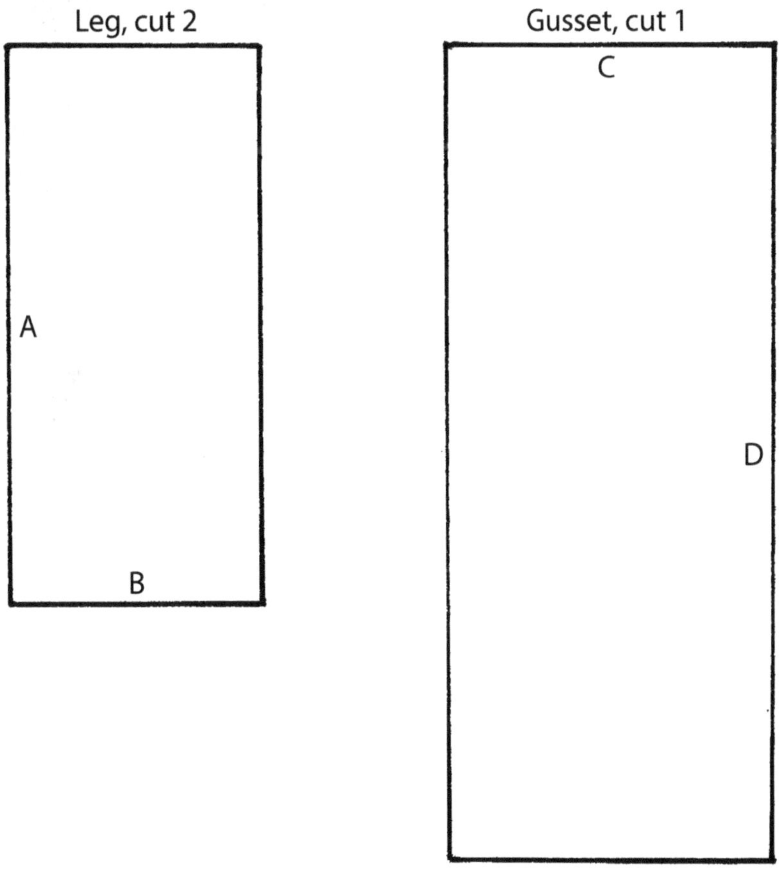

Berber dress from Morocco

8 One-piece Garments

Some tribal dancers prefer a more covered garment style. Others are looking for costumes suitable for folkloric style presentations. Still others are looking for costumes to wear to historical re-enactment events. For all of these dancers, a body-covering garment such as a *khaftan* or *tunic* may be the answer. There are many different options in shape and cut to create numerous different looks. In this chapter, I will introduce the main stylistic groupings of costume that provide the coverage many dancers require.

Body covering styles are the garments of choice for dancers who are drawn to the tribal style because of its historical allusions. The use of traditional textiles and ethnic jewelry, which are stylistically related to older historical models, appeal to historical re-enactors. The tribal style provides a formula for creating a Middle Eastern costume with a historical flavor by using currently available materials. You can find a wide array of tribal variations at Renaissance festivals and at SCA events.

However, the tribal style is a composite of various parts from all over the Middle East. As such, it is not an accurate representation of a style from any particular tribal group or even region. To assist dancers who are looking for information on putting together a more historically accurate costume, I have compiled an extensive bibliography and have included a brief guide to research in Appendix E.

When making these garments, it is strongly recommended that you make a sample out of inexpensive fabric. Pattern making can be a hit or miss proposition. Getting it right with an old sheet, for example, will allow you to create your final masterpiece in that authentic Syrian *ikat* with little waste and frustration. When you have finished your sample garment, put it on and dance. Some of these costume styles are limiting. You may find that a khaftan covers too many of your movements, or that a tunic needs a huge gusset to allow you to lift your arms. Just standing in front of the mirror will only tell you part of the story. If you are going to a multi-day event where you will be wearing your costume for hours, remember to test movements that you will run into through the day. For example, can you maneuver your costume while in a Porta-Potty?

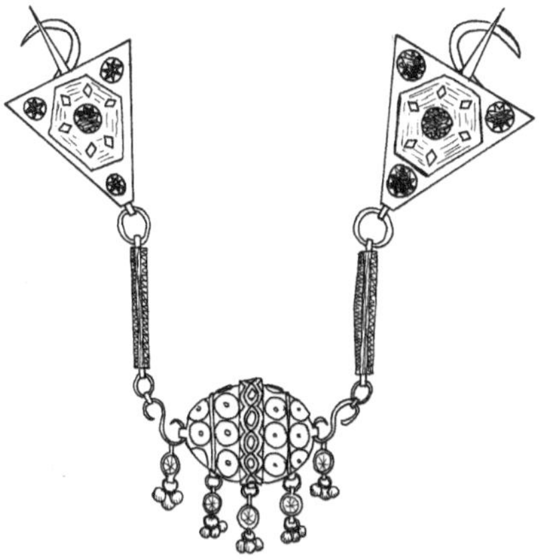

Fibula

Wrapped Garments

One of the oldest garment types are the wrapped garments of the Berber tribes across North Africa. These costumes originally were brought to the area by the Romans were composed of a long rectangular length of fabric that is wrapped around the body and pinned in place at the shoulder. The fibula serves as a closure, holding the garment closed while decorating it all at the same time.

These garments can be worn over a fitted tunic or a choli. Once they are wrapped and then pinned, a belt is tied around the waist. This belt can be as simple as a single cord or as ornate as a full tribal belt. Frequently, the cloth is taller than the woman wearing it. It is then pulled up and allowed to drape over the level of the belt.

Khaftans

A garment worn throughout North Africa and Arabia is the khaftan. These areas do not have a long tradition of representational art, so there are few representations of this type of garment. This garment, which is also commonly called a robe, is closed down the middle and is slipped on over the head. It is composed of a central panel, a pair of side panels, sleeves and gussets for movement.

Robes and similar garments are worn by tribal peoples throughout Arabia, Syria and Central Asia. Each region has its own particular cut, such as the *thobe* of Saudi Arabia which is a very wide and flowing variation of the khaftan. There are also complex traditions of surface design and embroidery such as the very distinctive gowns worn by Palestinian women feature elaborately embroidered decorative bands and panels in bright colors on a field of black.

The traditional cut of this garment in long narrow panels is the result of the narrow ground looms used by bedouin women to weave the fabric. For the most traditional look, select rough or coarsely spun fabrics in natural hues and use narrower panels. However, with fabric available in greater widths, variations of the khaftan can be made without the side seams.

Step 1: The first measurement is the width of your shoulders. You may want to expand this slightly, especially if you have full hips. This is the first mark on your central panel (A).

Step 2: Next, take a measurement from your shoulder to the top of your foot or the floor. This is the length of your garment and becomes the second line in your central panel (B).

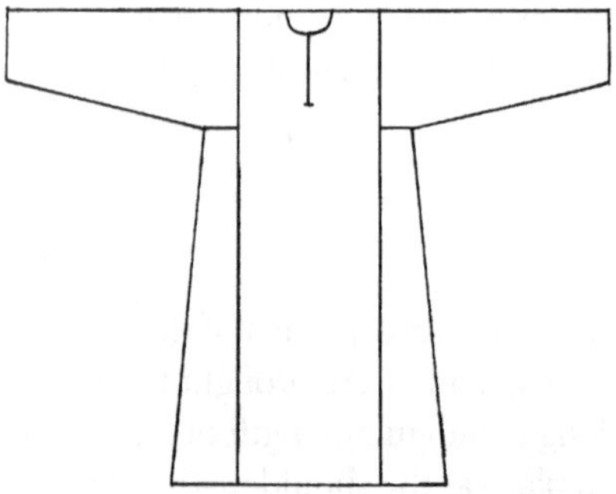

Step 3: Measure the length of your arm (C). Measure the fullest part of your arm as well, this is usually the biceps plus one to two inches for ease (D). Use these two marks to form a rectangle. Most dancers like to taper their sleeves to give them more shape. Use the measurement of your wrist plus ease, or anywhere from 2 to 6 inches (5–15 cm), depending on your look. Divide this number in half and draw out from the center length line on either side of your sleeve hem (E).

Step 4: To raise and lower the arm efficiently, make a gusset. A gusset is a triangular wedge of fabric that is sewn into the underarm of the garment to allow for movement. Although gussets can vary in size and finding the size and shape that works best for you takes some trial and error, try making a diamond. The cross measurements on a standard gusset are 4" by 5".

Step 5: To add fullness to your garment, you can add one or more side panels. These can be simple rectangles that go all the way up to the under arm areas. These are very much dependent on the style of garment you are making, how much fullness you want to achieve and what fabric you are making your piece out of. Make sure the center panel widths plus the side panel widths (A+A+G+G+G+G) are enough to go around your chest. To calculate (F), take (D) and divide it by 2. Subtract that from (B).

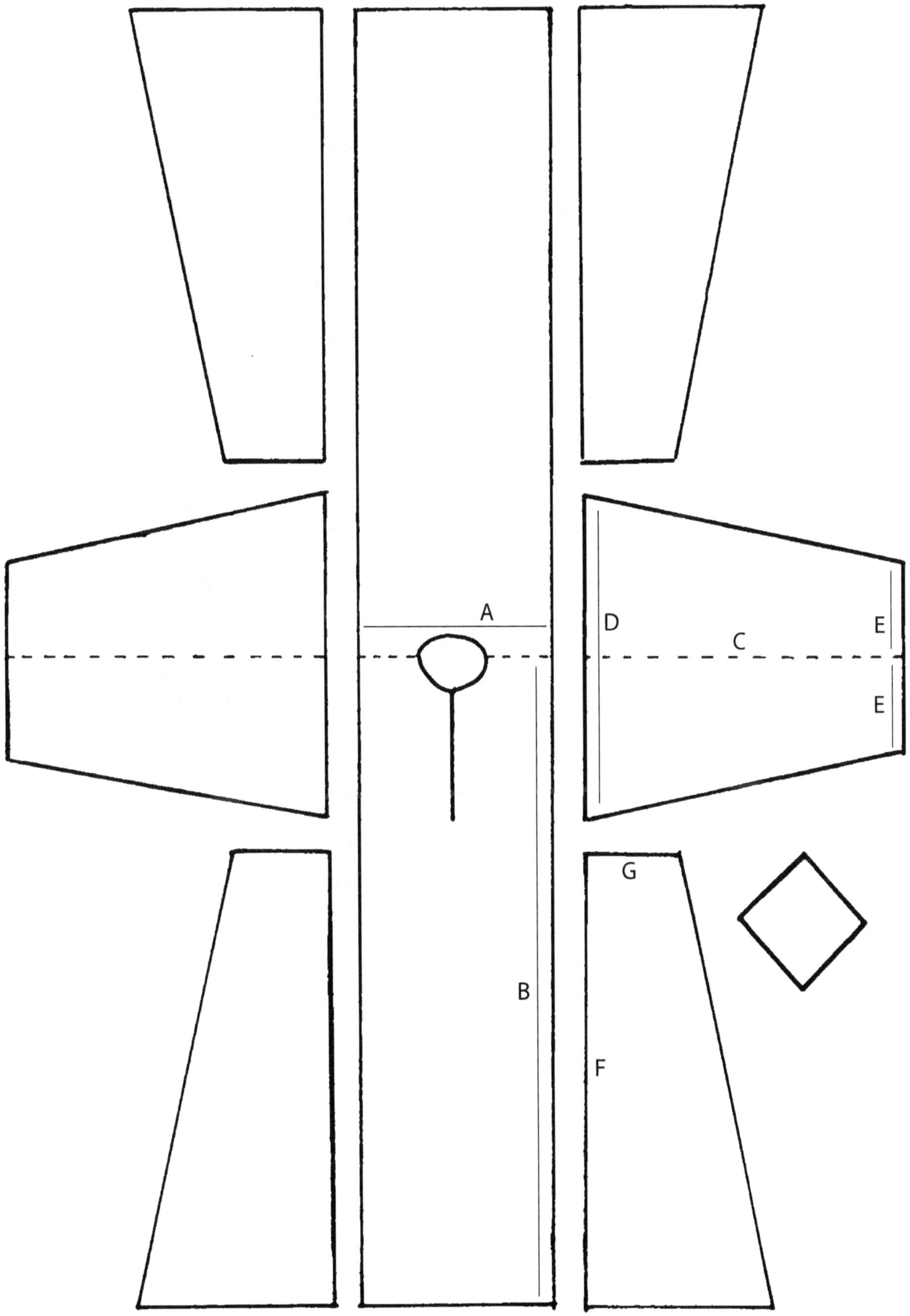

Pattern layout for a basic khaftan.

Anteri/Yelek

For many dancers who perform in historical environments, the wearing of historical reproductions is the main goal of their costuming. Many dancers who do historical re-enactments integrate these historical influences into a tribal ensemble. Two of the best-documented historical garments are the Turkish *anteri* and *yelek*. Examples of these garment types have survived and remain the holdings of museums such as the Topkapi-Saray in Istanbul and the Victoria and Albert Museum in London.

The anteri is a sleeved robe that was worn by both men and women during the reign of the Ottomans (1299–1923) and similar garments were also worn by people in Persia under the Safavyd dynasties (1501–1723) as far east as the Mughul Empire in India (1528–1858). All of these cultures produced manuscript illuminations that document the evolution of these traditional garments.

The anteri, known by many names including the Turkish coat and the gawazee coat (especially when the neckline is cut to go under the bustline), is a long fitted robe that closes up the center front. It has sleeves that are tapered, although they frequently are split to allow the lower half of the sleeve to swing free. The garment is simply composed of a front and back, sleeves and gussets under the arms to allow freedom of movement. The garment flares from the waist or the hips down to create more fullness at the knee or ankle.

The yelek, which traditionally was worn under the anteri, is a sleeveless vest that is cut along similar lines. If you want your anteri or yelek to be form fitting, you can shape the sides to match the curve of your body. You can also install a central back seam and curve it to fit the back.

Step 1: Begin by taking your chest measurement and adding 3–5 inches (7–12 cm) to it, depending on the amount of fullness desired. Divide this number in half to create your shoulder line (A). Remember, you can always take it in easily; it's more difficult letting it out.

Step 2: Next, draw a line from shoulder height to your knee or to the floor (B). If you would like the garment to be constructed without a shoulder seam line, double this length, drawing in the shoulder line at the midpoint. If you position this line in the center of line (A), it will also serve as your opening.

Step 3: Mark your hip line (C).

Step 4: Decide how full to make the skirt. Draw in a line representing half of the total circumference of your skirt (D). Make sure to center this line.

Step 5: Connect the hip line to the skirt (E).

Step 6: Make the sleeves following the directions for the khaftan. If you want a slit in your sleeves, they generally are positioned on the front of the sleeve as illustrated (F).

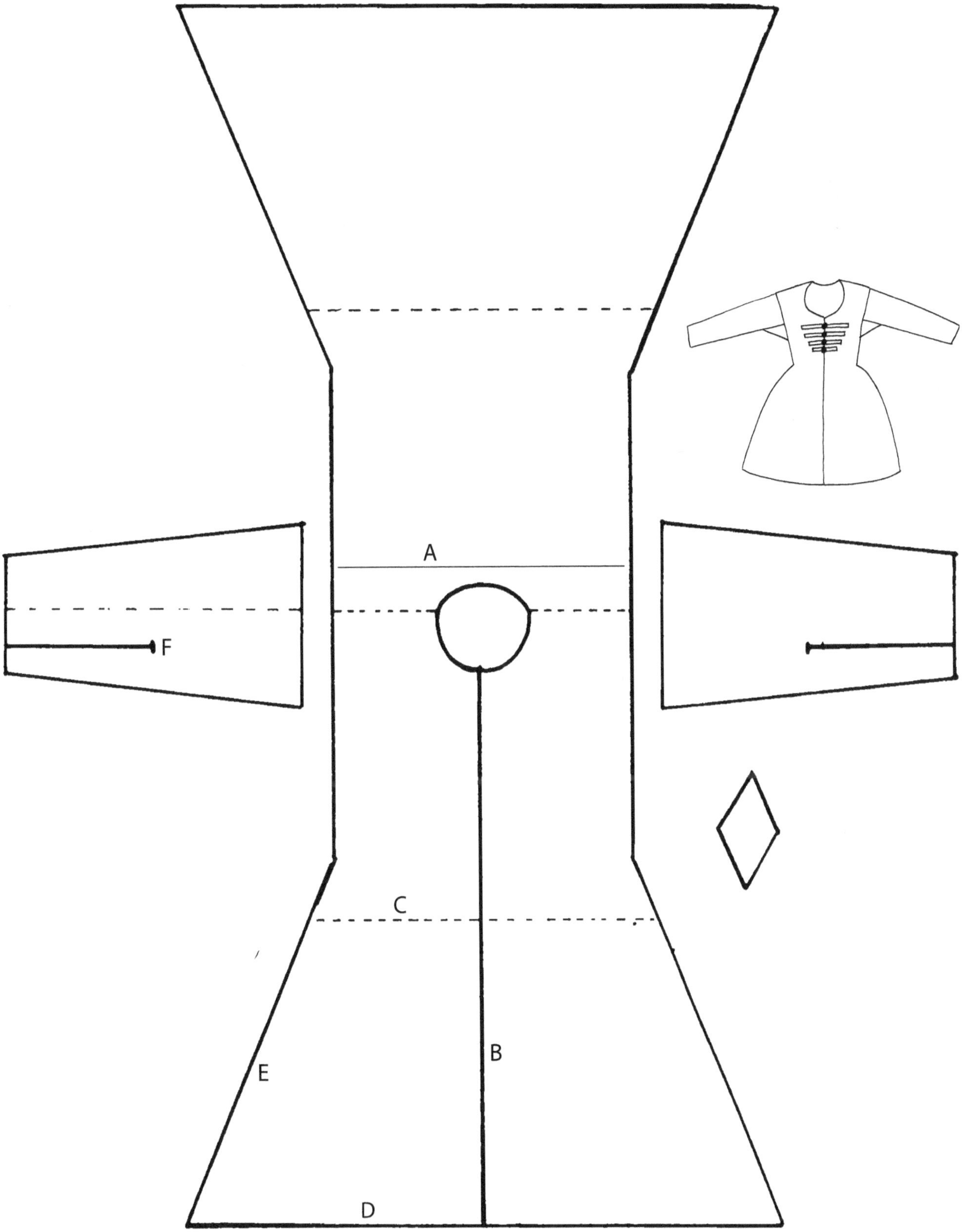

Pattern layout for a basic anteri or yelek.

Tunic

The tunic is a T-shaped garment that is composed of a rectangle of cloth, sleeves and a gusset. This style of garment has been found throughout the Near and Middle East and is a design of great antiquity. Variations of the tunic have been uncovered in Coptic burials in Egypt as early as the 4th century BC. The simple construction make it a good project for even a novice pattern maker or seamstress. These make a very comfortable costume and when worn over the pants and belted looks equally attractive on male and female dancers alike.

Because of the simplicity of the line, the fabric choice really impacts on the look of the finished garment. They can be adapted to many different uses with a few changes in the shape of the neckline, the type of fabric and the length of the garment. It can become a simple shift to wear under a yelek or anteri when made from a lightweight fabric such as a batiste. In contrast, it can be made from a dark heavy fabric to give the look of a more substantial robe.

This is a simple garment and requires only a few basic measurements to make. Like all ancient garments, the tunic is composed of simple rectangles. You will need your chest measurement, hip measurement, arm length and biceps.

Step 1: Measure your hips or chest and select the largest measurement. Add two or more inches (this determines the fullness of the garment) to this measurement and then divide by two. This becomes your shoulder line (A).

Step 2: Measure down from the top of your shoulder to the desired length (B).

Step 3: Mark your hip level (C) and then mark where you want your tunic to stop (D). This can be your hip line, above or below as suits your design.

Step 4: Measure your arm length and add 2 inches or 5 cm (E).

Step 5: Use your biceps measurement plus two or more inches to determine your sleeve width (F). You can taper your sleeve by using a smaller measurement for the hemline (G). Make sure that this is wider than your wrist to allow your hand to pass through.

Step 6: A gusset is necessary to allow freedom of movement for the arms. A standard gusset is approximately 4" tall by 5" (10×13 cm) long. The size of the gusset will depend on many factors including how high you like your arms to go up and what kind of fabric your costume is made of. A sample garment is critical. If your arm won't go up high enough, make the gusset deeper. If you have too much bulk in the underarm area, reduce the height. If you want to move your arm forward and backwards more, extend the length of the gusset front to back.

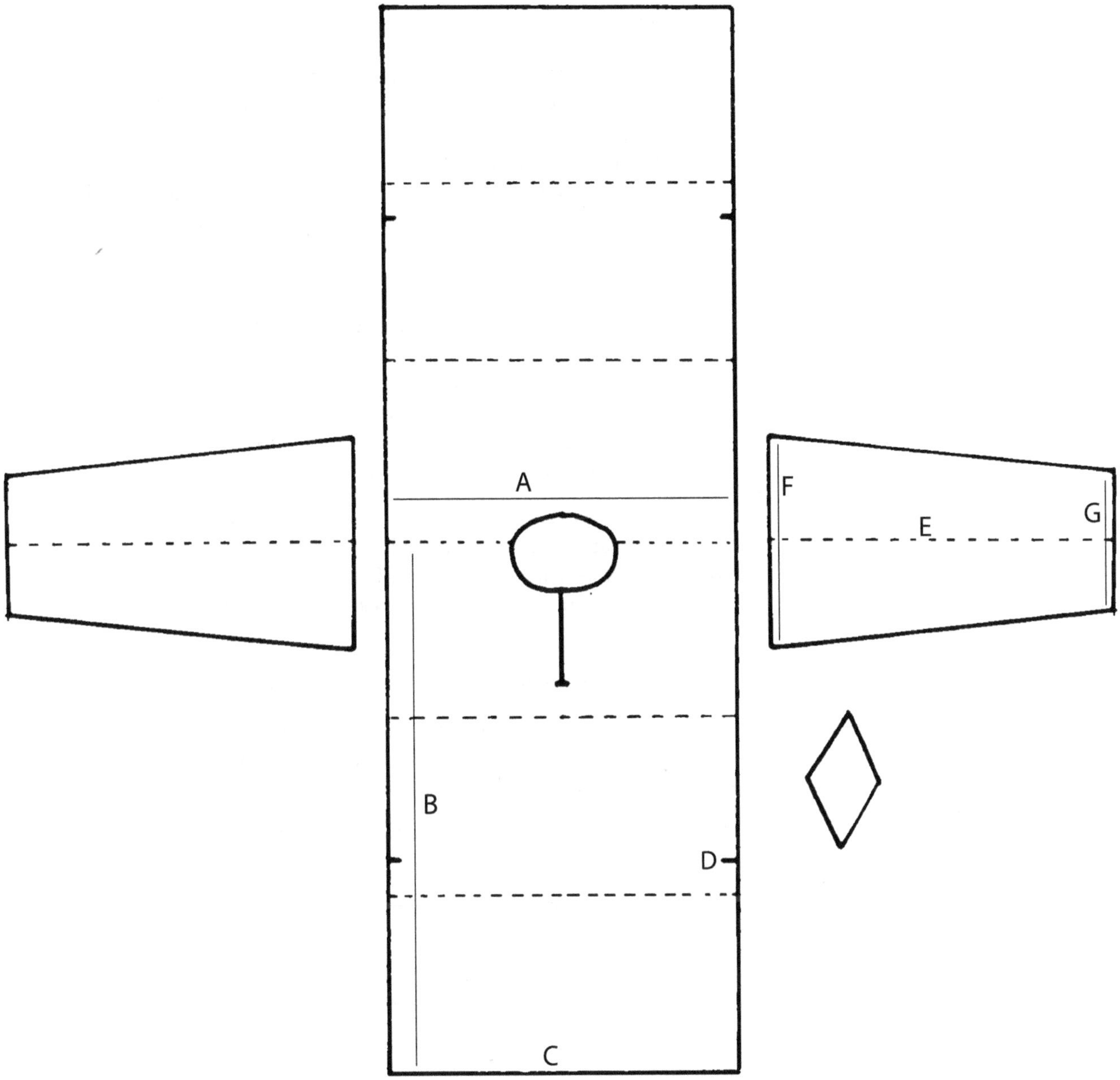

Pattern layout for a tunic.

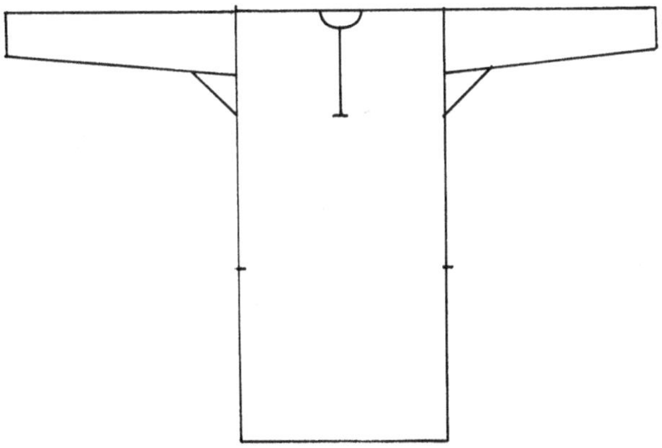

Wraps

If you are going to be performing in an outdoor venue, an article of clothing that will be an essential item in your wardrobe is a coat, wrap or cape. This garment will serve as your outermost layer and can be either plain or ornate depending on your taste and the venue. It should be sturdy enough to protect you from the elements while remaining lightweight enough to easily pack up if the weather is fine. You may also want your cover-up to be large enough to fit over your costume to cover it entirely, if necessary for a dramatic entrance.

There are many pattern companies that sell cape patterns. Capes come in a wide variety of shapes and styles, and, when made from fabric with good drape and flow, can be used during performances in lieu of a veil. Capes can be as simple as a circle of fabric. They can have all sorts of design features worked into the garment from shaped shoulders to hoods, from slits for arms to linings with pockets for carrying important items.

The easiest cover up to make is a modified cocoon wrap. This is an easy garment to make. It looks extra fabulous when made from a large printed cloth. Try this with an Indian printed bedspread for a relaxed and fun look. For a petite woman use a twin sized cover, for a lager woman, a full sized works well.

Step 1: Start with a length of fabric the width of your arm span.

Step 2: Fold the fabric lengthwise and stitch from approximately 5 inches (12 cm) below the fold to the corner of the fabric. Turn the fabric and continue to sew approximately 20 inches (60 cm).

Step 3: Turn the fabric and attach a weight to the corner. This can be a coin, a piece of jewelry or a tassel.

Step 4: Wear by slipping your arms through the stitched holes.

Capes can be made in any length.

The easiest wrap to make begins with a rectangle
and ends up looking smashing!

Step 1

Step 2

9 The Skin

Beneath all of the elaborate layers of costuming elements required to create the tribal style lies the most important element: *you!* To finish the "look" many dancers have moved beyond the conventional high glamour styles of cosmetics favored by their rhinestone and sequin-wearing sisters and have turned their attentions towards more traditional cosmetic techniques. From wearing replicas of facial tattoos to the use of complex henna designs or even permanent tattoos, the body itself becomes a canvas for design and self-expression.

Cosmetics

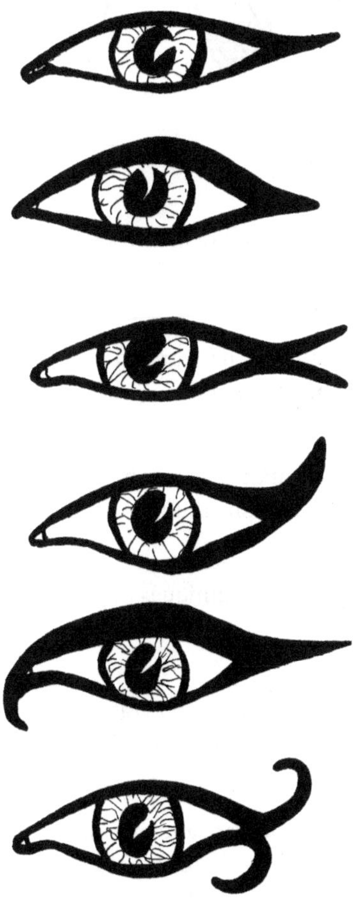

There are many ways to apply cosmetics, thousands of products on the market, but there is only one you. Your skin is precious and deserves the best quality cosmetics that you can afford. It is a financial investment and a selection of products that are tailored to your specific needs will save you time in swift applications and produce a more polished look. But unlike costume pieces, which you can resell if they don't work out, cosmetics are harder to return and recoup the losses. So, when experimenting, find a place that will accept returns or will replace a product that does not work for you. Have your face "done" by a consultant at a makeup counter, not because the look will be suited for performance, but because you will discover how your skin reacts to the products before you make a significant investment.

What constitutes the "tribal look" in cosmetics? There are many subtle permutations that vary from dancer to dancer. After observing a plethora of dancers over the years, I have constructed the following list of characteristics that routinely appear in their makeup programs. All of the major cosmetic brands produce products that can be combined to create these looks, so be sure to experiment until you find what works best for you.

Fair Complexion: Many dancers favor a matte finish look to their foundation, while others prefer a more dewy look. In either case, the foundation layer smoothes out the complexion, evens the tones of the skin and provides a base upon which to apply other cosmetics. Over the years, I have seen a few dancers use darker shades to add color to their skin as if they have been walking through the desert themselves. Make sure that what ever color your choose complements your actual facial tones. One option is using a skin bronzing product to give that added glow of simulated sun.

Dark Eyes: Stylized eyeliner is one of the most dramatic and characteristic elements of the tribal face. *Khol*, which has been used since the dawn of time to rim the eyes, is now made from safe ingredients by cosmetic manufacturers. While many dancers still use khol products, it can contain impurities that can lead to infection. Make sure you purchase real khol, or any other cosmetic product, from a reputable source. Experiment with styles and shapes, extending the line out away from the eye into different positions. The application of eye shadow and the use of mascara all add to the effect of a dramatic, deep and dark eye.

Tribal Tattoos: Many tribal dancers utilize the facial tattoos worn by numerous nomadic and rural peoples of the Near and Middle East. These markings are used to show clan affiliations and, among tribal dancers, they become part of their performance persona. Eyeliner can be used to draw these designs onto the face along the nose, across the cheekbones or on the chin. A good source of design inspirations for tribal tattoos are old copies of *National Geographic* magazine and in anthropological discussions of tribal peoples.

Bindies: These little facial embellishments are worn by women from India and come in numerous styles, shapes and forms. They can range from inexpensive to wonderful works of art that can draw the audience's eye directly towards your own. There are many places to purchase bindies. You can find them with your favorite belly dance vendor or, if you live in a large city, at your local Indian grocery store. They can be inexpensive, with multiple bindies coming on the same card, or luscious confections created with tiny pearls and gems. Bindies are reusable and can be reapplied with spirit gum or eyelash glue.

Tips on Cosmetics

Here are some general tips on cosmetics.

- Invest in good quality makeup applicators. A set of brushes will last for years when taken care of properly. Look for good brushes in art supply stores as well as at the makeup counters.
- Practice, then practice some more. Even if you have an established look, don't let it stagnate. Play with colors, application techniques and surface design effects.
- Test-drive your makeup. Wear your performance makeup to class to make sure that the designs and products don't melt under the heat of dancing.
- Go see a makeup artist. Try any tips, hints or techniques of people who have the best "looks." Don't be shy! Ask other dancers about the products they use or how they use them.
- Powder is your friend. Remember to use powder to set your foundation well before building up additional layers of cosmetics over it. Subsequent layers will adhere better and will be less likely to run.
- Toss out old cosmetics that you don't use. Mascara and eyeliner should be no more than six months old. Other cosmetics should be tossed out on a yearly basis to avoid infections caused by bacterial growth.
- Avoid sharing cosmetics, especially products that come into contact with your eyes.

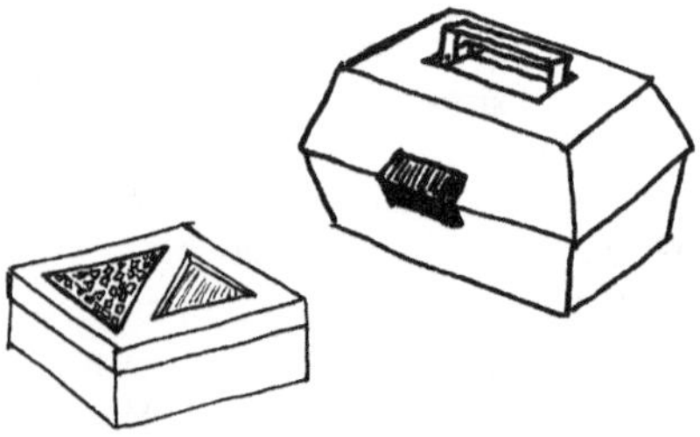

Store your tools and cosmetics in a portable box for those performances that take you away from home.

Mehndi

The art of using the ground leaves of the henna plant to dye the skin is known by many different names throughout Africa, the Middle East and India. Most commonly in the United States, it is referred to simply as *henna* or by the Indian name *mehndi*. It is a centuries-old practice that has been used ritualistically for celebrations, medicinally to treat a wide variety of ailments and as a natural coolant for the skin. Designs were originally applied using a small pointed stick, but contemporary mehndi artists use either a cone made of plastic sheeting or a plastic squeeze bottle with a very fine tip.

The henna plant originated in Egypt along the banks of the Nile. Mummies, dating back to the Early Kingdom have been found with hair and nails dyed using henna. Contemporary henna designs vary from region to region, from bold geometric designs of Africa to the subtle delicate floral patterns of India. The patterns can appear nearly anywhere on the body, but the preferred areas are the arms, hands, neck, shoulder area and feet.

Mixing the Dye Paste

There are many different subtle variations to the basic recipe for making henna paste. Like cooking, the exact ingredient list and the quantity will vary. The amount of liquid necessary will depend on the dryness of the henna powder.

The henna can be purchased from your favorite belly dance supplier, via mail order from a vendor online, or at a local Indian or Middle Eastern market in your area. You want to make sure that the henna you use is as fresh as possible and is ground into a very fine powder. You may need to grind your henna further using a mortar and pestle and sift it. You can use a section of a pair of nylons or a piece of gauze pulled tightly over a bowl.

Basic Henna Recipe

3 teaspoons of henna, finely ground and sifted
1 teaspoon of oil
1 cup of liquid

Next the oil is added. Generally, it's best to add the oil a drop at a time, blending gently with a spoon. There are several different types of oil that can be used in the henna process. Clove oil and mustard oils are favored by many although eucalyptus oil is generally gentler on the skin. Make sure to test the type of oil you are planning on using to prevent possible allergic reactions.

Finally, the liquid is added to the mixture a few drops at a time. You want to make sure that you do not make the paste too wet or the designs will spread. You also want it to be moist enough to squeeze easily from the cone or bottle. It takes some experimenting and practice to achieve a consistency that is somewhere between toothpaste and readymade frosting.

The liquid you choose to use will affect the depth of color of the henna. If water is used, the henna design will be pale. Tea or coffee brewed until it is strong and dark will give the henna paste a darker richer color. Coffee will add a deep, dark brown color, while black tea will sometimes enhance the natural ruddiness of the henna. Brew the tea or coffee the day before to get the optimal coloring results.

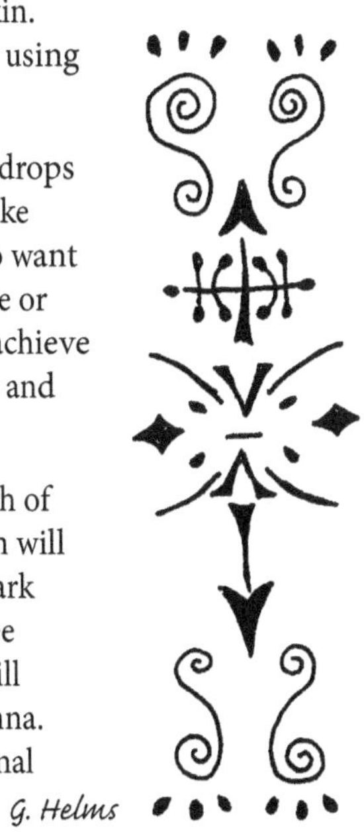

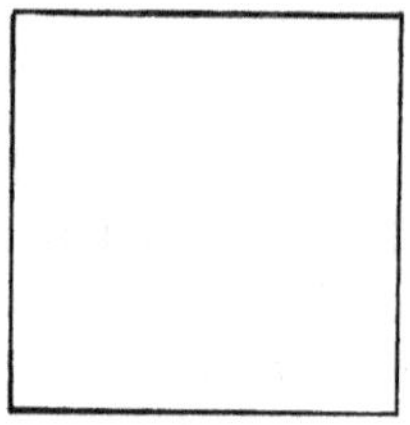

Step 1: Start with a square sheet of plastic.

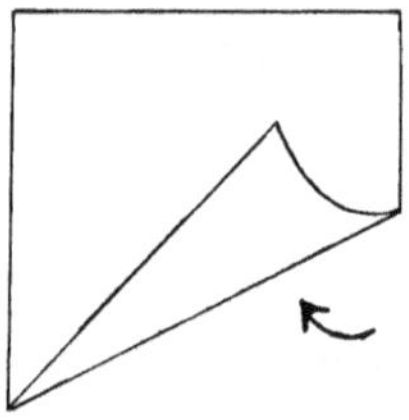

Step 2: Roll the sheet into a cone.

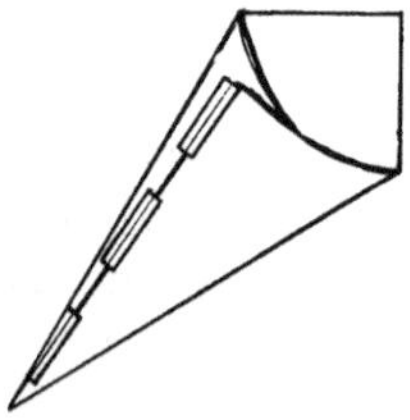

Step 3: Tape the cone closed.

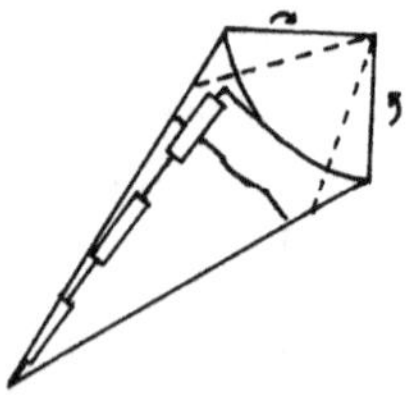

Step 4: Fold the top sides inward.

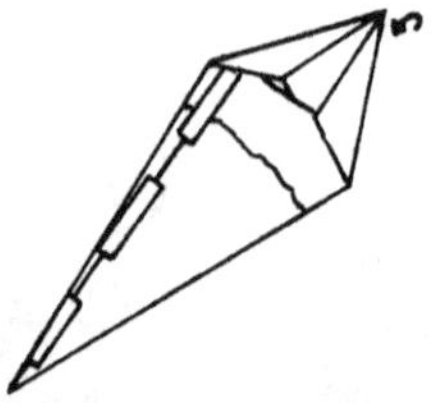

Step 5: Roll the top down.

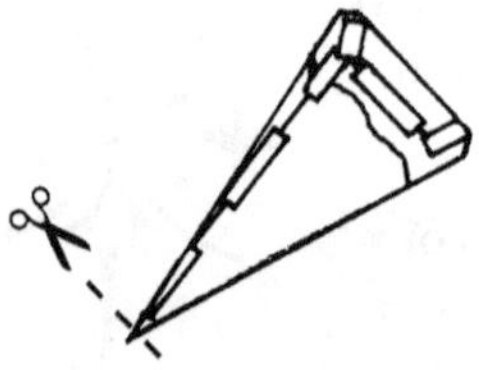

Step 6: Tape the top closed and cut the tip off.

Henna can be kept in the refrigerator for several days but it will deteriorate in strength without showing much change externally. You can freeze henna to preserve it for several weeks or months if need be. However, it needs to be at room temperature when applied. If the paste is chilled, you will not get as dark or rich a color.

Applying the Paste

Henna is generally applied with either a cone or a plastic squeeze bottle. Bottles can be purchased in the dye or paint sections of a large craft center or art store. Look for small bottles that have fine tips. Some can be found with tips as narrow as 2 mm and these can be used to make very delicate lines. They are reusable but have to be thoroughly cleaned after use to prevent the narrow opening from clogging.

Another alternative is to use a cone. Following the same basic principles of the pastry bag, the cone has the benefit of being inexpensive and disposable. See instructions to the left for making the applicator cone. Filled with henna, is held in much the same way as a pastry bag is and is squeezed to get a good flow going. You can practice on a piece of wax paper until you get the hang of it. Scrape the henna off the paper and reuse it for practice until it dries.

Once the paste is applied, a mixture composed of one teaspoon of sugar and the juice from half a lemon is applied over the top of the henna design. This helps set the paste firmly. The longer the paste remains on the skin, the darker the resulting design will be. Applying heat to the design by holding it near a candle or incense will help make the design a deeper color. Some henna designers will use a heating pad to rest a hand on, for instance, to aid in the darkening process.

When the henna is dry and begins to flake, the best way to remove the paste is to scrape it off with the edge of a spoon or other utensil. Once the henna has been removed, a layer of eucalyptus or olive oil is applied to the skin to help set the design. Be gentle with your mehndi and it will last for several weeks.

Drawing the lotus

Henna Designs

Henna designs are limited only by your imagination. There are numerous pattern books on the market due to the widespread interest in mehndi designs. Public figures, rock stars and actresses have been sporting henna designs for several years. The spotlight of attention may, at any moment, swing in another direction as styles fall out of favor. Now is the time to purchase books on mehndi design.

Each region has a particular flavor to the design motifs that are reflective of the styles of jewelry, textiles patterns and other decorative arts. Across North Africa, motifs are bold and geometric. In India, the designs are subtle and complex floral motifs. Experiment with designs until you find a style and technique that looks good and works for you.

The designs in this chapter and throughout the book may seem overly complex, but in reality they are built up from numerous small, easier strokes. Large patterns are built out of repetition starting either from one end, as in a boarder design, or they begin in the center and work outward, such as in a mandala pattern. For other designs that are free-form, pick a logical starting point. For instance, I like to begin a paisley design at the fullest part of the shape. Practice with designs to perfect your technique.

There are many places to find inspiration for mehndi designs. Clip art books full of traditional patterns are available and have the benefit of clean, clear, easy-to-follow directions. For more complex patterns, try looking in books on rugs and rug history for design inspiration. These books will frequently be accompanied by color photographs of rugs with pictorial glossaries that describe the design vocabulary of rug makers in different regions.

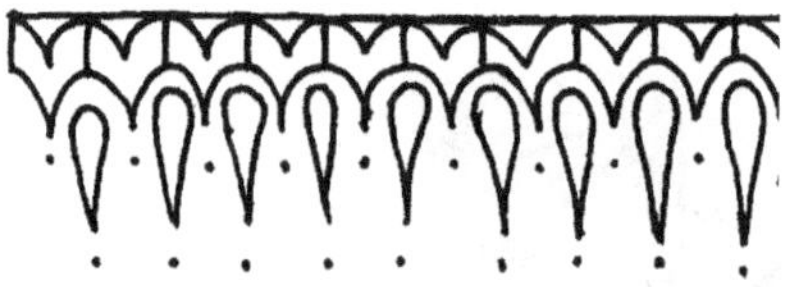

Henna Tips

Here are some ideas that will help streamline your henna process:

- Exfoliate the areas you are going to henna to remove any dry skin. This will help to preserve the design.
- Oil the area after the henna is removed. Olive oil works very well and is less expensive than eucalyptus or other types of oils.
- Harsh cleaning products containing AHA ingredients will remove your mehndi designs. Henna will react adversely with sunscreen and tanning products as well. If you have patterns on your hands, wear gloves when washing dishes to protect your art.
- Ritualize the mehndi process by having special tools, such as a special bowl and spoon. It also helps to have all of your tools gathered and set out ceremonially. Light a candle, burn some incense and put on some relaxing or energizing music. Invite friends over to enjoy the moment.
- Henna can be a messy process, so keep cleaning and wiping supplies nearby. Toothpicks and cotton swabs will help scrape and shape henna lines. If you are using a squeeze bottle, keep a pin or needle handy to clear the nozzle. Paper towels, warm moist washcloths and a bowl of water will keep the work area neat and tidy.

- Don't have time to mix up a batch yourself? Experiment with some of the henna products that come premixed in a tube. While henna in this form is generally of weaker strength, it does save time when you are starting out and experimenting.
- Cold will slow down the henna's ability to set properly. If you keep your henna refrigerated allow the paste to return to warm temperature before applying to the skin. You can refrigerate henna up to three days or freeze for several weeks before the potency diminishes.

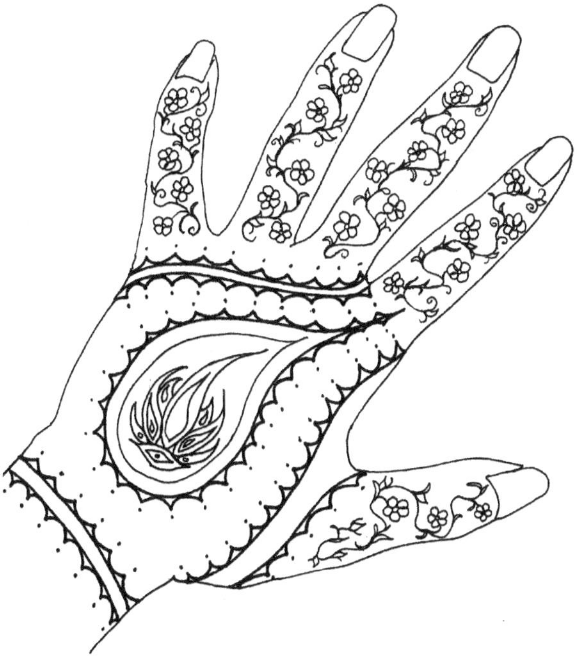

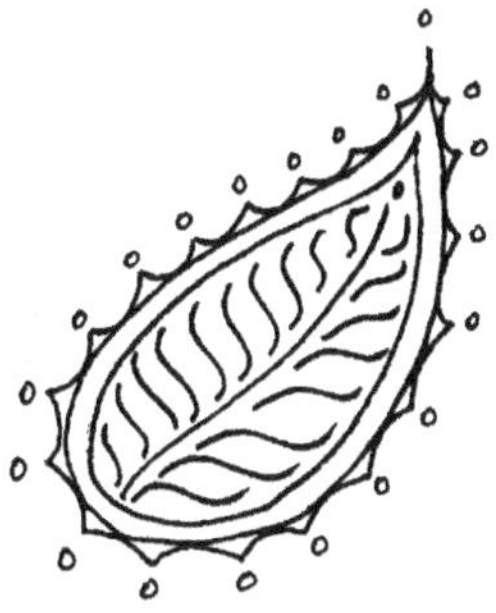

A Appliqué Techniques

The appliqué technique is one of the most popular surface design treatments used in India today. Not only does it allow the designer to pick and choose from a variety of different colors and patterns of fabric, it also allows textiles to be recycled. Textiles, for most of the mankind's history, have been a precious commodity due to the amount of intensive labor that went into the production of even the smallest amount of cloth. Today, fabric is readily accessible but the traditions of using appliqué still remains.

One of the most distinctive design elements, appearing in the work of Ribari women of India, is the highly contrasting sawtooth applique treatment. Frequently stark white against a background of red, blue or black cloth, this treatment is used as a decorative boarder or band and can be found on cholis, skirts, cuffs of pants and in household textiles such as the toran and chakla.

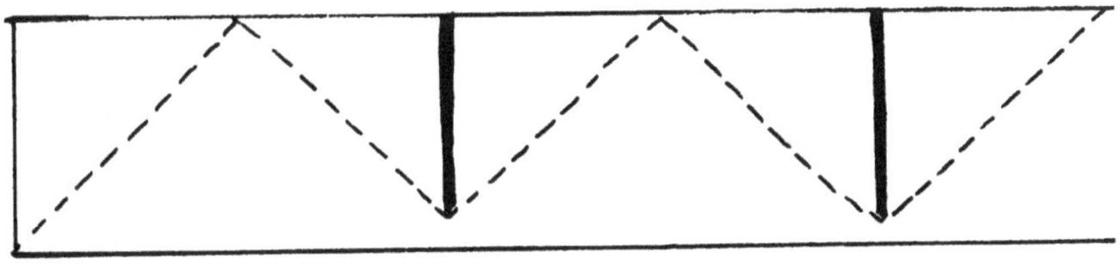

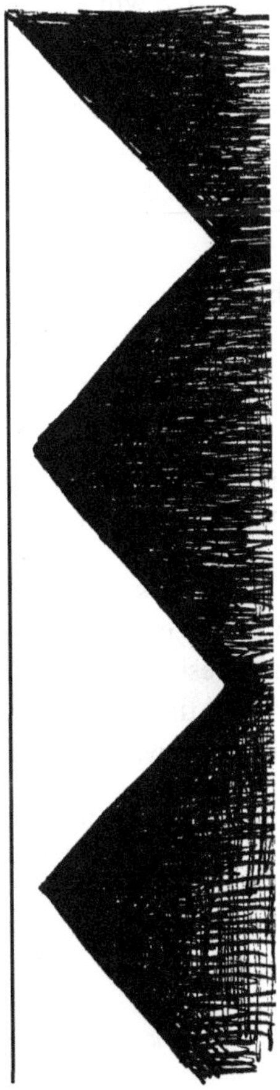

Step 1: Measure out the length and determine the height of the points. Next determine the width of your points. This is easiest if divisible by an even number. So, if you have a piece that is 12" (30 cm) long, make the points an inch (2 cm) high and 2 inches (5 cm) wide. This will create six points within the length you require.

Step 2: Draw planning lines onto your cloth using a fabric marking pen or a piece of chalk. Cut on the solid line leaving 1/8" (3 mm) to link the points together.

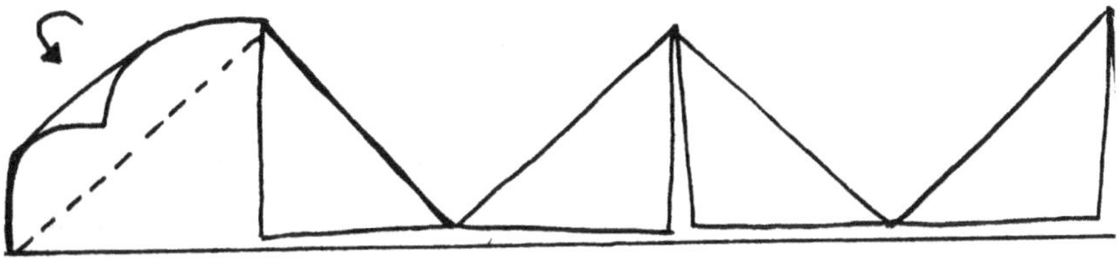

Step 3: Fold on the dotted lines and press firmly with a steam iron set the proper temperature for the textile you are using.

Step 4: Lay the applique into place and either top stitch using a sewing machine or use a hand sewing technique. Slip stitching will be invisible, while an edge stitch will add another decorative element. If you do not like to sew, you can apply this with a commercially available fusible adhesive product and using an iron. There are several products on the market, make sure to read the manufacturer's directions and test a sample before applying.

B Tassel Making

The bouncing, free-flowing movements created by tassels are one of the hallmarks of the tribal style. Tassels are easy to make although they can be quite time consuming. There are as many different methods for creating tassels as there are costume makers. There are several good books on tassel making currently out on the market. However, it is a simple process that requires only a pair of scissors, yarn and something to wrap it around.

However, if you are planning on making a quantity of tassels that match, a template will help you achieve uniform size and shape. Keeping a sample tassel available and comparing it with your work will also help maintain uniformity. Templates can be made out of any firm cardboard, but foam core makes the most rigid base to wrap your tassels. The following technique has successfully made thousands of tassels, but feel free to modify these directions to suit your individual needs.

Step 1: Cut your template. You will want to use a template that is approximately an inch (3 cm) longer than your final tassel length. Two templates are included to the left to get you started.

Step 2: Prepare the template. Cut a length of yarn between 5" and 6" long (12–15 cm) and wrap it around the board and either tape it down or tie knots in the ends to catch in the slots. This piece of yarn will form the top loop.

Step 3: Wrap. Tie a knot in the end of your yarn and catch it in the slot of the template. Wrap the yarn around the template until you have reached your desired thickness. For best results try not to pull tightly on the yarn. If you are looking for tassels that absolutely match, you can count the number of wraps and write it onto the template.

Step 4: Make the top loop. Release the thread for the top loop and pull it to the top of the tassel. Tie it double knot it for strength. This loop should be loose enough to be able to pull another piece of yarn through, but firm enough to hold the tassel together.

Step 5: Release the tassel. Using a pair of scissors, cut along the bottom edge of the tassel to release it from the board. Rotate the top loop downwards, so the knot is buried underneath the tassel.

Step 6: Make the collar. With another short piece of yarn (5" to 6", 12–15 cm), wrap firmly around the head at the position desired for the collar and tie. Take your collar thread and begin wrapping around the collar until it is as wide and firm as you desire for your look. Tie off and bury within the skirt of the tassel.

Step 7: Trim. Shape the bottom of your tassel, making it a uniform length. You may want to fluff your tassel once or twice to relieve any tension that may have been applied to the thread during wrapping, and then trim one final time.

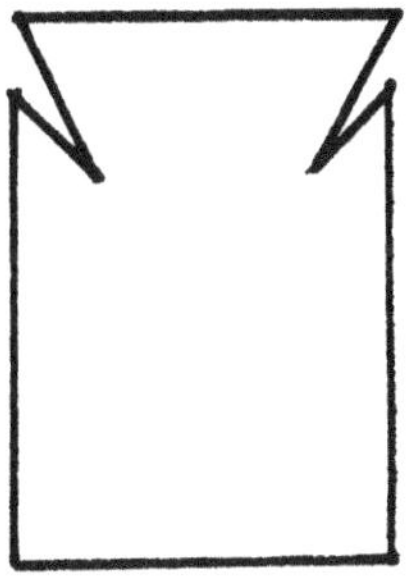

Step 1

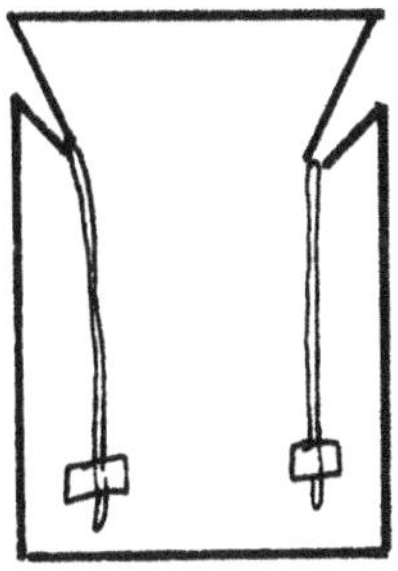

Step 2

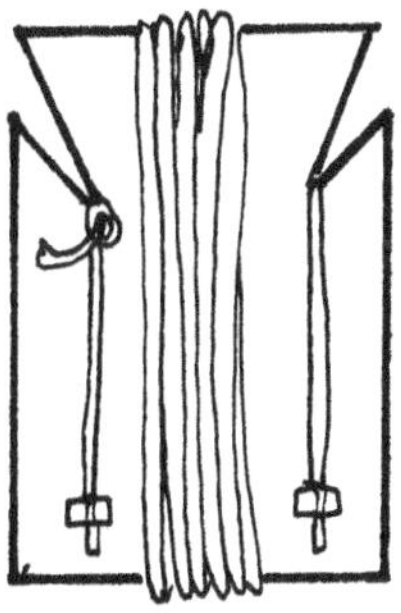

Step 3

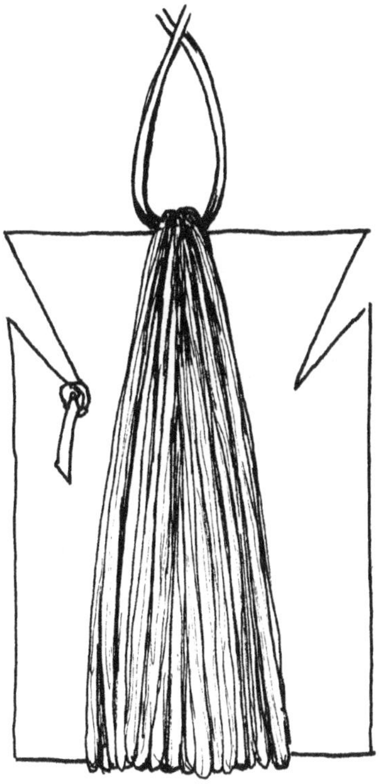

Step 4

Step 6a

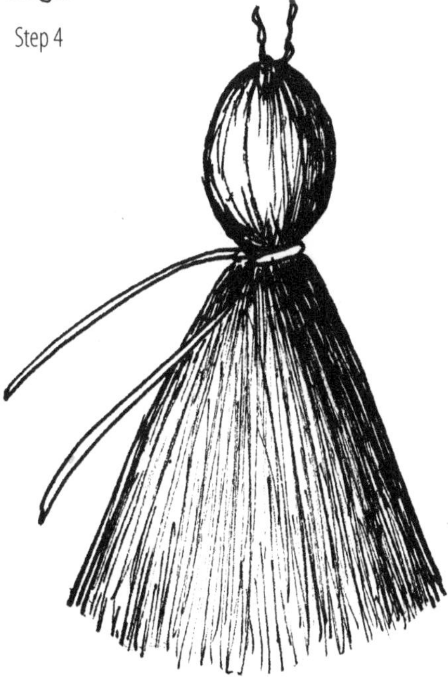

Step 6b

Step 6c

Shi-sha

The easiest and most common shi-sha technique is the chain stitch. It is also the most delicate and mirrors can come loose easily.

Shi-sha is an embroidery technique and is thought to have originated in India. It begins appearing in artistic depictions such as Moghul manuscript illuminations that date to the sixteenth century. Folk wisdom has passed on the romantic story that the wife of Shah Jahan, who erected the Taj Mahal, invented the technique. However, it is more likely an ancient tradition that originated in the Indus region, possibly in the Gujarat, Kutch and Saurashtra areas. Shi-sha can appear as random designs scattered across the surface of a cloth, or worked into dense complex embroidery patterns.

There are several different methods for applying shi-sha and countless variations on the formation of the stitches. Below I have included directions for the two most common variants in shi-sha application: the embroidered and the layered methods. While you are practicing, I recommend acquiring a general embroidery reference book or stitch encyclopedia to give you more ideas for stitch variations. Remember that shi-sha application is time-consuming, so experiment and plan your projects wisely.

Embroidered Shi-sha

Step 1: Glue your mirror down using a washable fabric adhesive. This will protect the mirror from parting company with your garment. It also holds the mirror in place while you are doing the embroidery over it.

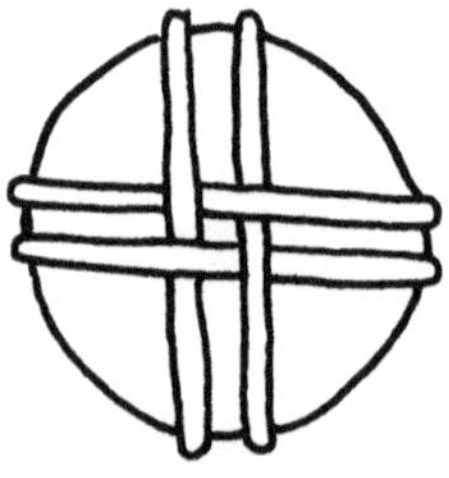

Step 2

Step 2: Form the base stitches. These should be firm. If they are too loose, the embroidery over it will sag, potentially allowing the mirror to fall out. If the base stitches are too tight, the exposed part of the mirror will be quite small. Finding the perfect tension for your style of embroidery takes practice.

Step 3: Work around the perimeter of the mirror, catching and wrapping the base threads and pulling them taught. The goal is an even smooth shape to the opening. Most shi-sha work features a round opening; however, squares and diamonds are also popular.

Step 4: Work completely around the mirror and finish the work by knotting on the backside below the mirrored surface.

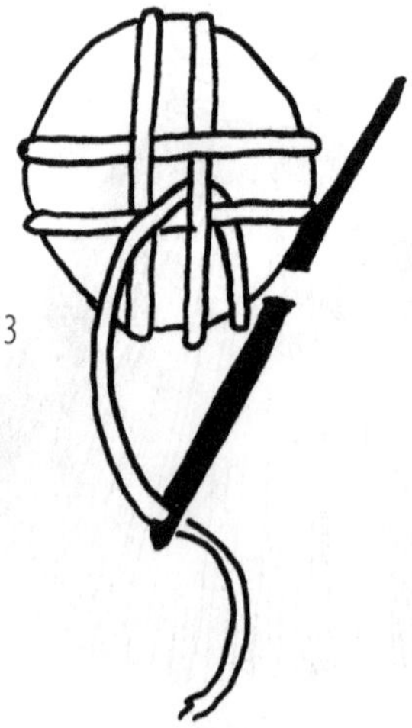

Step 3

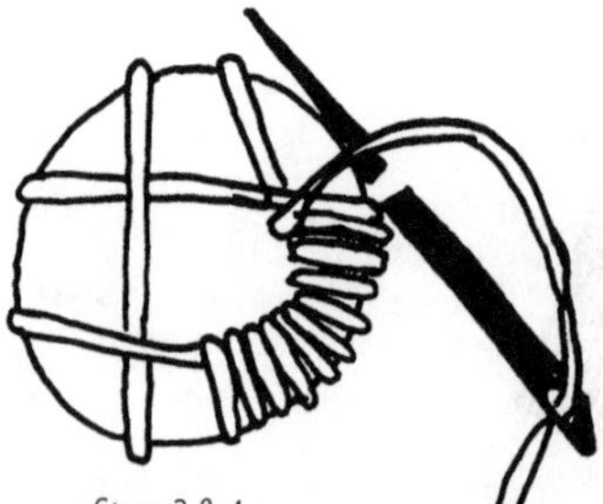

Steps 3 & 4

Example of finished product

Sandwiched Shi-sha

Step 1: Glue your mirror down using a washable fabric adhesive. This is a very critical step in this type of application. You will glue down all the mirrors in the area being worked. Once you lay over your top fabric and begin stitching, you will have great difficulty adding or removing mirrors from below.

Step 2: Lay your covering fabric down over the top of your mirrors. Baste or top stitch by hand around the perimeter of each mirror about 1/8" to 1/4" (2–5 mm) away from the outer edge. Use a thread that contrasts so you can easily see where you have sewn or incorporate this basting stitch into your final design. If you don't want it to show, and you want to save time, you can baste using a matching thread to the background fabric.

Step 3: Cut an X in the fabric directly above the center of the mirror. The legs of the X should be approximately half the diameter of the mirror. If you are using a very large mirror, you may want to make the X bigger, in which case you want to make sure the X doesn't get closer to the edge of the mirror than 1/8" (2 mm).

Step 4: Fold the tabs under, revealing the mirror below. You may need to clip the points off these tabs so that they do not make a bulge under the fabric. Once the tabs have been turned under, you can proceed with embroidering around the edge of your pieces using an embroidery edge stitch.

Step 3

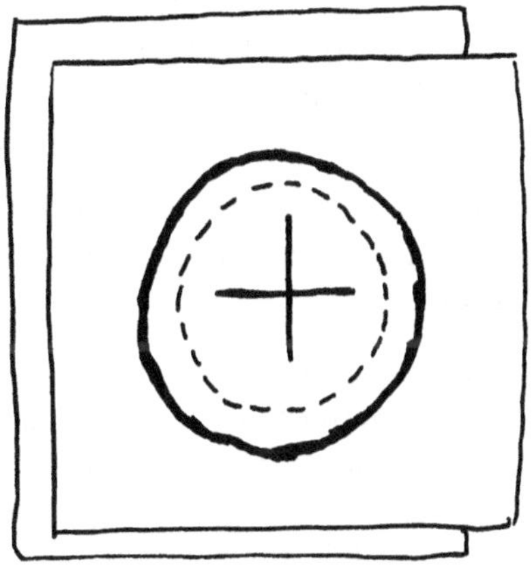

Step 4

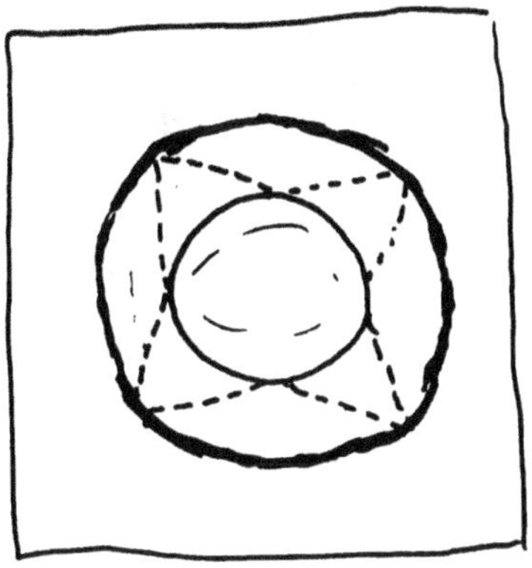

Finished shi-sha

D Care and Handling

Tribal costumes can be created that are easy to care for. The absence of sequins, glass beads and rhinestones eliminates many of the cleaning challenges that are common for standard belly dance costumes. However, tribal and traditional handmade folk textiles can require special care and handling to preserve their beauty.

I encourage all dancers to develop a routine for post-performance inspection, repair and cleaning. The better the quality of the care you give your costume, the longer it will look good. After investing resources, time and money into developing a wardrobe of costume parts and pieces, caring for them will preserve your investment for many hours of performance. Every performer has her own techniques for costume care and preservation. Ask your favorite dancer how she keeps her costumes in show condition. Below are some helpful tips to get you started.

Invest in pieces that are machine washable. Tribal style costuming has the benefit of using natural materials for many of the garment pieces. When selecting pants, consider the care factor that is required by some fabrics. Rayon, a popular choice for pants, for instance, sometimes requires hand washing and should be allowed to air dry. Pants made out of linen, cotton, hemp or ramie, however, can be machine-washed and -dried, saving lots of time.

Avoid putting garments made with Lycra/Spandex into a dryer with heat. This fiber is heat-sensitive, and is major component of many stretch cholis. Increase the life of your garment by allowing it to air dry.

Test for colorfastness before washing garments. If you are making a costume piece, test a scrap. If you have purchased a garment, try testing in an unobtrusive location before laundering the entire garment. For embroideries, you can test by laying a clean white cloth or paper towel that's been dampened onto the surface of the object and pressing firmly. Pull the towel up and inspect for traces of color. If any color appears, assume the textile is going to run. Some textiles will, unfortunately, be unwashable.

- For garments that are not safe to wash, you can use a several techniques for "freshening" them up between performances.
- Swipe with the surface of the textile with a clean soft brush. This will brush away any dried particles from the surface.
- Spot clean with water and soap, not detergent. Rinse by blotting.
- Lay natural fiber textiles out in the sun.
- Use a vacuum cleaner. Using a nozzle covered with a piece of cloth, you can run it over the surface of the textile, sucking up dirt. This works especially well with a less powerful hand-held vacuum.

- Spritz garments with a solution of one part vodka to one part water. This is especially effective at removing odors. Also try commercial products to remove odor.

Keep a repair kit ready and use it. At the minimum, keep an assortment of threads to match your costumes, needles, scissors, a good, clear fabric adhesive to secure knots and stitching on the underside of garments, and straight pins and safety pins to keep pieces together while repairing them. Include the phone number of a good seamstress for the repairs that seem hopeless.

Protect your garment. Practice performance routines that include the use of a sword which can inadvertently snag or tear garment pieces. The same holds true for candles or other burning objects. When performing, steer clear of tables with candles and, if you are dancing in a restaurant, beware of how close you are to such dishes as "flaming cheese." When dancing around a fire, remember that textiles reach out much farther than your body, so know your limits to protect not only your garment but yourself, as well.

Use linings for non-washables. Garments that cannot be washed should have linings that are designed for easy removal. When you are making a garment from scratch, put the lining in last and do not sew surface embellishments to both layers. Belts, bras and cholis made from traditional textiles will all last longer when lined.

Avoid wearing the same costume pieces over and over again. By having more garments that you can rotate through performances, you will extend the life of each individual garment. This will also give you enough down time so that you can make repairs, change linings and allow traditional textile pieces to rest.

Store your costume pieces in a moisture-free environment. Use a desiccant such as silica gel to eliminate mold and mildew growth by pulling moisture from the air. Include a fabric bag of baking soda or cornstarch to absorb odors.

E Guide to Research

The tribal style is very appealing to dancers who are interested in historical research and re-enactment. The traditional textiles, natural fibers and surface design treatments have been passed on through the generations. The origins of many of these techniques and processes are firmly rooted in a distant past.

Are tribal styles historically accurate? Can these garments be adapted to create a costume suited for wear to historical events? To fully consider these questions, one has to invest a considerable amount of time and energy to excavating historical documentation. To further these goals, I have created a brief study guide to research in the field of Middle Eastern costume that may point in some useful directions for your further studies.

Illustration drawn from Mughal manuscript illumination, dated c. 1586–1590.

Narrow Down Your Subject and Cast a Wide Net

Beginning with a broad-reaching search for all of the information about Middle Eastern costume would be an overwhelming project for even the most dedicated scholar. So, instead of trying to collect an all-encompassing collection of facts, try to narrow your search down to a particular location and historical moment. It is far easier, for instance, to focus on costumes in India between 1500 and 1600 than to attempt to survey all of the Middle East in that century or to try to do a complete survey of Indian costume across the centuries.

However, looking for all of your sources in costume, textile and art history sources would be very limiting. Once you have defined your topic, expand your research to include cultural and social histories, literature and other contemporary writings, decorative arts and architecture. Books of these kinds will frequently feature reproductions of maps, manuscript illuminations and images of other decorative arts as a form of visual documentation to support the text.

Primary vs. Secondary Sources

Being able to evaluate the quality of a source is essential when performing research. There are two major types of source materials: primary and secondary. Knowing what you are looking at will allow you to make judgements about the quality of the information.

Primary sources are any writings, objects or artistic creations made within the culture during the period in question. This is the most important factual information but it frequently needs interpretation. Secondary sources are later writings that interpret, define, categorize or extrapolate from the primary source material. The book you are currently reading falls into this category. Contemporary researchers, historians and authors have pre-processed the historical information for you.

But before you just "trust" what has been written, find out who the leading researchers are in your field of interest and consider their credentials. The support of major museums, academic appointment and extensive publications are all good signs that the researcher is a reputable source. However, just by looking over a book you can get some clues to the value of the source, as all good secondary sources will:

- Refer to their primary source material.
- Cite their sources in the form of footnotes, endnotes or in text citations.
- Include a bibliography or works cited page.

Without documentation of the supporting primary evidence, the information presented in a secondary source is considered anecdotal and suspect.

Extrapolation

This concept is critical to engaging in living history or historical reproduction. Costumes and textiles do not handle the ravages of time well. Some environments and cultural practices have allowed some textiles and garments to survive. However, these garments are a very small sample of what was worn and does not usually reflect the clothes worn by the general population.

Consequently, some extrapolation must occur if a reproduction garment is to be created. Most surviving garments were rare and treasured because of sumptuous materials or because of rarefied ownership. Frequently, these garments only exist due to burial, or have been held in the treasuries of palaces and holy centers. Reproducing them faithfully would be an inaccurate representation of the garments of common people, but this is a useful clue for extrapolation. Ask yourself questions like:

What materials would an ordinary garment have been made out of?

What changes would have been made for the cut of the garment?

What embellishment techniques would common people use?

If the garment is from a later period, what would have been worn in the eras before?

If the garment is from an earlier period, how would the style have changed as time progressed?

An example of extrapolation can be found in North Africa, which was settled by the Greeks and subsequently by the Romans. The Roman style of dressing was the toga: a long rectangle of fabric was wrapped around the body and held in place by a pair of pins known as *fibula*. There are Roman sculptures that survive in Carthage and Tunis depicting women wearing these garments as late as the fourth century AD.

Across North Africa today, a similar style of wrapped garment is worn by women. The ancient name for the pin that hold the garment together, the fibula, is still in use. Now consider, if that garment was being worn in the fourth century, and it's being worn in the twenty-first century, was it being worn in, say, the tenth century? Perhaps a wrapped garment held in place by a fibula?

Methodology

Use every source available at your disposal. Major universities have larger collections of books, while inter-library loan programs can bring the titles you need to your local library. Ask your library to find out what services they offer.

Create a bibliography and keep updating it as you find information. Use the bibliographies of other authors to search out their sources and work backwards. Eventually you will find your way towards the primary source material. Keep track of what you have looked at and make notes about the quality of the information. This will be an invaluable tool as your research progresses and you start sharing information with other people.

Make the Internet your friend. Many resources are now available online. From major library indexes to pages devoted to virtually every topic under the sun, explore the offerings available. Make use of this wonderful tool not only for performing research, but for contacting others researching your field as well. Information only becomes powerful when you share it with others.

Primary Source Materials

Surviving textiles and costume pieces. There are many textiles that have survived and appear in a variety of different sources. Museum collections and exhibition guides are your best bet. General survey books on Islamic arts will frequently feature textiles and costuming as well, though not as extensively.

Manuscript illuminations. The art of the book was commonly practiced in the major courts throughout the Middle East. You can find illuminations in general survey books of Islamic arts, books specifically on manuscript illumination and sometimes even in translations of Islamic texts with the original illuminations reproduced.

Travel diaries. Hunt down translations of travelogues written during the years of your research study. While their accounts are second-hand, many take time to describe what they see, the people they met and occasionally will go into detail about the costumes.

Photography. If your period of choice is the late nineteenth or twentieth centuries, you can use photography as part of your documentation. Remember that although photographs show you *exactly* what the camera saw, the pictures can be every bit as contrived as paintings from the same era. Postcards and photography in travel magazines such as *National Geographic* give a glimpse into the costume and dress of women during these eras.

Fine and decorative arts. Explore the world of art looking for paintings and sculpture that depict clothed individuals. There are several excellent survey books on Islamic art available. Also look at works by the Orientalists, a school of painting, photography and writing that started in the late eighteenth century in Europe.

Historical Resources

All the books in the first section of the bibliography are museum and exhibition guides that are excellent sources for images of costumes, cultural items and household goods. Each of these books puts the material you are looking at into a historical perspective and include bibliographies to form a basis for further exploration.

Look at costume history books. There are few books devoted specifically to costume and textile history. You will have to be patient in your search. Costume also falls under the domain of anthropology and you can find some excellent historical material written by cultural anthropologists.

The Best Book on Middle Eastern Women's Costume

Scarce, Jennifer. ***Women's Costume of the Near and Middle East.*** Unwin Hyman: London 1987. (Only goes back as far as the late 13th century.)

Other Essential Books for the Costume or Textile Historian

Baker, Patricia. ***Islamic Textiles.*** British Museum Press: London 1995.

Askari, Nasreen and Rosemary Crill. ***Colors of the Indus.*** The Victoria and Albert Museum in conjunction with Merrell Holberton Publishers: London 1997.

Gillow, John and Nicholas Barnard. ***Traditional Indian Textiles.*** Thames and Hudson 1993.

King, Donald. ***Imperial Ottoman Textiles.*** Colnaghi: London 1980.

Rogers, J. M. ***The Tpokapi Sara Museum, Costumes, Embroideries and Other Textiles.*** Thames and Hudson: London 1986.

Spring, Christopher. ***North African Textiles.*** British Museum Press: London 1995.

Woven from the Soul, Spun from the Heart: Textile Arts of Safavid and Qajar Iran, 16th–19th Centuries. The Textile Museum: Washington, D.C. 1987.

Other Top Picks

Cultural history is very important as well. Invest in a good general book on Islamic Art and try to locate an art historical resource for your country of choice as well.

Irwin, Robert. ***Islamic Art in Context: Art, Architecture and the Literary World.*** Harry N. Abrams:New York 1997.

Lewis, Barnard. ***The World of Islam: Faith, People, Culture.*** W. W. Norton & Co.: New York 1992.

F Bibliography

Many people have trouble finding sources for historical research on the subject of Middle Eastern costume. Below is a portion of the bibliography that I use. Check your local public library, favorite bookstore or the nearest college or university library. There are many excellent articles in magazines and journals on these subjects that are too numerous to include here.

Exhibition Guides and Cultural Survey

This section contains survey books that cover textiles, costuming and jewelry. Most of these books are exhibition guides and are quite well written and feature excellent photography.

Ammoun, Denise. ***Crafts of Egypt.*** American University of Cairo Press: Cairo 1991.

Basilov, Vladimir. ***Nomads of Eurasia.*** University of Washington Press: Seattle 1989.

Jereb, James F. ***Arts and Crafts of Morocco.*** Chronicle Books: San Francisco 1995.

Khalter, Johannes. ***The Arts and Crafts of Syria.*** Thames and Hudson: London 1992.

Khalter, Johannes. ***The Arts and Crafts of Turkestan.*** Thames and Hudson: New York 1983.

Khalter, Johannes. ***Heirs to the Silk Road: Uzbekistan.*** Tames and Hudson: New York 1997.

Topham, John. ***Traditional Crafts of Saudi Arabia.*** Stacey International: London 1981.

Costume and Textile History

This section contains books that cover various aspects of the history of textiles and costumes. Most focus on the Middle East while others are general survey books that touch on a wide variety of topics. Costuming books go out of print rapidly and you may have to resort to inter-library loan to get a peek at some of the books listed below.

Alkazi, Roshen. ***Ancient Indian Costume.*** Art Heritage: New Delhi 1983.

Ambrose, Kay. ***Classical Dances and Costumes of India.*** A. & C. Black: London 1950.

At the Edge of Asia: Five Centuries of Turkish Textiles. Santa Barbara Museum of Art: Santa Barbara, CA 1983.

G. Helms

Askari, Nasreen. ***Uncut Cloth.*** Merrell Holberton Publishers: London 1999.

Askari, Nasreen and Rosemary Crill. ***Colors of the Indus.*** The Victoria and Albert Museum in conjunction with Merrell Holberton Publishers: London 1997.

Baginski, Alisa. ***Textiles from Egypt, 4th–13th Centuries.*** L.A. Mayer Memorial Institute for Islamic Art: Jerusalem 1980.

Baker, Patricia. ***Islamic Textiles.*** British Museum Press: London 1995.

Bebfoughal, T. ***Les Costumes Feminins de Tunisie.*** Enterprise Nationale des Arts Graphiques: Reghaia 1983.

Besancenot, Jean. ***Costumes of Morocco.*** Kegan Paul International: London 1990.

Bhushan. ***Costumes and Textiles of India.*** Taraporevala's Treasure House of Books: Bombay 1958.

Bijutsu, Indo Senshoku, and Kokyo Hatanaka. ***Textiles Arts of India: Kokyo Hatanaka Collection.*** Chronicle Books: San Francisco 1996.

Biswas, A. ***Indian Costumes.*** Publications Division, Ministry of Information and Broadcasting, Govt. of India: New Delhi 1985.

Boucher, François. ***20,000 Years Of Fashion.*** Abrams: New York 1987.

Boulanger, Chantal. ***Saris: An Illustrated Guide to the Indian Art of Draping.*** Shakti Press International: 1997.

Bunt, Cyril G. E.. ***Persian Fabrics.*** Textile Book Service: Plainfield, NJ 1963.

Burnham, Dorothy K. ***Cut My Cote.*** Royal Ontario Museum: Ontario 1973.

Centre des Arts et Traditions Populaires. ***Les costumes Traditionnels Feminins de Tunisie.*** Maison Tunisienne de L'edition: Tunis 1970.

Clothing and Difference: Embodied Identities in Colonial and Post-Colonial Africa. Hildi Hendrickson, edt. Duke University Press: Durham 1996.

Crill, Rosemary. ***Indian Ikat Textiles.*** Weatherhill: London 1998.

Das, Sukla. ***Fabric Art: Heritage of India.*** South Asia Books 1992.

Elson, Vickie C. ***Dowries form Kutch.*** Museum of Cultural History, University of California: Los Angeles 1979.

From the Far West: Carpets and Textiles of Morocco. Textile Museum: Washington 1980.

Guy, John. ***Woven Cargoes: Indian Textiles in the East.*** Thames and Hudson 1998.

Gillow, John and Nicholas Barnard. ***Traditional Indian Textiles.*** Thames and Hudson 1993.

Harvey, Janet. ***Traditional Textiles of Central Asia.*** Thames and Hudson:London 1996.

King, Donald. ***Imperial Ottoman Textiles.*** Colnaghi: London 1980.

Kumar, Ritu. ***Costumes and Textiles of Royal India.*** Manson & Woods: 1999

Laver, James. ***Costume & Fashion: A Concise History.*** Thames and Hudson: London 1985.

Lynton, Linda. ***The Sari, Styles, Patterns, History, Technique.*** Harry N. Abrams: New York 1995.

Mackie, Louise W. ***The Splendor of Turkish Weaving: An Exhibition of Silks and Carpets of the 13th–18th Centuries.*** The Textile Museum: Washington, D. C. 1973.

Maeder, Edward. ***Hollywood and History.*** Thames and Hudson/Los Angeles County Museum of Art: Los Angeles 1987.

Markaz al-Funun wa-al-Taqalid al-Sha'biyah. ***Les Costumes Traditionnels Feminins de Tunisie.*** Maison Tunisienne de L'edition: Tunis 1988.

Martin, Richard and Harold Koda. ***Orientalism: Visions of the East in Western Dress.*** Metropolitan Museum of Art: New York 1994.

Mayer, L. A. Mamluk ***Costume; a Survey.*** A. Kundig: Geneve 1952.

Museum of International Folk Art. ***A Portfolio of Folk Costume, Volumes One and Two.*** Museum of New Mexico Press: New Mexico 1971.

Naik, Shailaja D. ***Traditional Embroideries of India.*** South Asia Books: Columbia, MO 1996.

Kapur, Chrishti R. and Amba Sanyal. ***Saris of India: Madhya Pradesh.*** South Asia Books: Columbia, MO 1989.

Rajab, Jehan S., ***Palestinian Costume.*** Kegan Paul International: London 1989.

Rivers, Victoria Z. ***The Shining Cloth.*** Thames and Hudson: London 1999.

Reswick, Irmtraud. ***Tradtional Textiles of Tunisia and Related North African Weavings.*** Craft & Folk Art Museum: Los Angeles 1985.

Rogers, J. M. ***The Tpokapi Saray Museum, Costumes, Embroideries and Other Textiles.*** Thames and Hudson: London 1986.

Ross, Heather Colyer. ***The Art of Arabian Costume: A Saudi Arabian Profile.*** Arabesque Commercial: Montreux, Switzerland 1981.

Scarce, Jennifer. ***Embroidery and Lace of Ottoman Turkey.*** Royal Scottish Museum: Edinburgh 1983.

Scarce, Jennifer. ***Middle Eastern Costume from the Tribes and Cities of Iran and Turkey.*** Royal Scottish Museum: Edinburgh 1981.

Scarce, Jennifer. ***Women's Costume of the Near and Middle East.*** Unwin Hyman: London 1987.

Spring, Christopher. ***North African Textiles.*** British Museum Press: London 1995.

Stillman, Yedida Kalfon. ***Palestinian Costume and Jewelry.*** University of New Mexico Press: Albuquerque, NM 1979.

Thomas, Thelma K. ***Textiles from Medieval Egypt, A.D. 300–1300.*** Carnegie Museum of Natural History: Pittsburgh, PA 1990.

Tilke, Max. ***Folk Costumes from East Europe, Africa, and Asia.*** A. Zwemmer: London 1978.

Uemura, Rokuro. ***Persian Weaving & Dyeing.*** Unsodo Publishing Co.: Kyoto 1962.

Weir, Shelagh. ***Palestinian Costume.*** British Museum Publications LTD: London 1989.

Woven from the Soul, Spun from the Heart: Textile Arts of Safavid and Qajar Iran, 16th–19th Centuries. The Textile Museum: Washington, D.C. 1987.

Yarwood, Dooreen. ***The Encyclopedia of World Costume.*** Bonanza Books: New York 1986.

Jewelry

Andrews, Carol. ***Amulets of Ancient Egypt.*** University of Texas Press: Austin 1994.

Andrews, Carol. ***Ancient Egyptian Jewelry.*** Harry N. Abrams: New York 1990.

Beck, Horace. ***Classification and Nomenclature of Beads and Pendants.*** George Shumway Publisher: York, PA 1981.

Borel, France and John Bigelow Taylor. ***The Splendor of Ethnic Jewelry.*** Harry N. Abrams: New York 1994.

Butor, Michel. ***Ethnic Jewelry: Africa, Asia and the Pacific.*** Rizzoli: New York 1994.

Boyer, Martha Haensen and Ida Nicolaisen. ***Mongol Jewelry.*** Thames and Hudson: London 1995.

Coles, Janet. ***The Book of Beads.*** Simon and Schuster: New York 1990.

D'Orey, Leonor. ***Five Centuries of Jewellery.*** Scala Books: Lisbon 1996.

Dubin, Lois Sherr. ***The History of Beads: From 30,000 B.C. to the Present.*** H. N. Abrams: New York 1987.

Evens, Joan. ***A History of Jewellery, 1100–1870.*** Dover: New York 1970.

Fisher, Angela. ***Africa Adorned.*** Harry N. Abrams: New York 1984.

Hasson, Rachel. ***Early Islamic Jewellery.*** Institute for Islamic Art: Jerusalem 1987.

Hasson, Rachel. ***Later Islamic Jewellery.*** Institute for Islamic Art: Jerusalem 1987.

Higgens, Reynold. ***Greek and Roman Jewellery.*** Methuen and Co. LTD.: London 1980.

Islamic Jewelry in the Metropolitan Museum of Art. Metropolitan Museum of Art: New York 1983.

Mack, John. ***Ethnic Jewelry.*** Harry N. Abrams: New York 1988.

Meilach, Dona Z. ***Ethnic Jewelry: Design & Inspiration for Collectors and Craftsmen.*** Crown Publishers: New York 1981.

Nigam, M. L. ***Indian Jewellery.*** Tiger Books International: Twickenham, UK 1999.

Ross, Calyer Heather. ***The Art of Bedouin Jewellery, A Saudi Arabian Profile.*** Arabesque: Frisbourg, Switzerland 1981.

Tait, Hugh. ***Jewelry, 7,000 Years.*** Abradale Press: New York 1991.

Untracht, Oppi. ***Traditional Jewelry of India.*** Harry N. Abrams: New York 1997

Woodson, Yoko et al. ***Beauty Wealth and Power: Jewels and Ornaments of Asia.*** Asian Art Museum of San Francisco: San Francisco 1992.

Belly Dance History and Instruction

Al-Rawi, Rosina-Fawzia, B. and Monique Arav. ***Grandmother's Secrets: The Ancient Rituals and Healing Power of Belly Dance.*** Interlink Publishing 1999.

Buonaventura, Wendy. ***Serpent Of The Nile: Women and Dance in the Arab World.*** Interlink Books: New York 1989.

Buonaventura, Wendy. ***The Serpent and the Sphinx.*** Lodon: Virago 1983.

Carlton, Donna. ***Looking for Little Egypt.*** IDD Books: Bloomington, IN 1994.

Dahlena and Dona Z. Meilach. ***The Art of Belly Dancing.*** Bantam Books: Toronto 1975.

Djoumahna, Kajira. ***The Tribal Bible.*** Kajira Djoumahna's Black Sheep Books, Bodywork and Bazaar: Santa Rosa, CA 1999.

Gioseffi, Daniela. ***Earth Dancing, Mother Nature's Oldest Rite.*** Stackple Book: Harrison, PA 1980.

Hobin, Tina and Kristyna K'ashvili. ***Belly Dancing: For Health and Relaxation.*** Focus Publishing: NY 1982.

Mishkin, Julie Russo. ***The Compleat Belly Dancer.*** Garden City: New York 1973.

Nieuwkerk, Karin van. ***A Trade Like Any Other: Female Singers and Dancers in Egypt.*** University of Texas Press: Austin, TX 1995.

Serena and Alan Wilson. ***The Serena Technique of Belly Dancing.*** Pocket Books: New York 1974.

Pattern making, Construction and Surface Decoration

Armstrong, Helen Joseph. ***Patternmaking for Fashion Design.*** Harper & Row: New York 1987.

Amaden-Crawford, Connie. ***The Art of Fashion Draping.*** Fairchild Publishers: New York 1995.

Bensussen, Rusty. ***Making Patterns from Finished Clothes.*** Sterling Publications: New York 1985.

Bensussen, Rusty. ***Shortcuts to A Perfect Sewing Pattern.*** Sterling Publications: New York 1989.

Brij Bhushan, Jamila. ***Indian Embroidery.*** Publications Ministry, Ministry of Information and Broadcasting, Govt. of India: New Delhi 1990.

Crutchley, Anna and Tim Imrie. ***The Tassels Book.*** Lorenz books: New York 1996.

Doyle, Tracy. ***Patterns from Finished Clothes: Re-creating the Clothes You Love.*** Sterling Publications: New York 1996.

El-Khalidi, Laila. ***The Art of Palestinian Embroidery.*** Al Saqi 1999.

Eaton, Jan. ***The Complete Stitch Encyclopedia.*** Quarto Publishing: London 1995.

Embroidery and Lace of Ottoman Turkey. Royal Scottish Museum: Edinburgh 1983.

Grewal, Neelam. ***The Needle Lore: Traditional Embroideries of Kashmir, Himachal Prdesh, Punjab, Haryana, Rajasthan.*** Ajanta Publications: Delhi 1988.

Holkeboer, Katherine Strand. ***Costume Construction.*** Prentice Hall: Englewood Cliffs NJ 1989.

Jaffe, Hilde. ***Draping for Fashion Design.*** Prentice Hall: New York 1993.

Johnstone, Pauline. ***Greek Island Embroidery.*** H.M.S.O.: London 1972.

Johnstone, Pauline. ***Turkish Embroidery.*** Victoria & Albert Museum: London 1985.

Kopp, Ernestine, et all. ***Designing Apparel Through the Flat Pattern.*** Fairchilds Publishers: New York 1991.

Morrell, Anne. ***Techniques of Indian Embroidery.*** B.T. Batsford: London 1994.

Paine, Sheila. ***The Afghan Amulet: Travels from the Hindu Kush to Razgrad.*** Michael Joseph: London 1994.

Readers Digest. ***Complete Guide to Sewing.*** The Reader's Digest Association, Inc.: Pleasantville, NY 1995.

Singer. ***Creative Sewing Ideas.*** Singer: Minnetonka, MI 1990.

Singer. ***Sewing Essentials.*** Singer: Minnetonka, MI 1989.

Singer. ***Sewing For Special Occasions.*** Singer: Minnetonka, MI 1994.

Taylor, Carol. ***Creative Bead Jewelry.*** Sterling Publishing, Inc.: New York 1995.

Taylor, Enid. ***Tassel Making for Beginners.*** Sterling Publications: New York 1998.

Weir, Shelagh. ***Palestinian Embroidery: A Village Arab Craft.*** British Museum: London 1970.

Welsh, Nancy. T***he Creative Art of Tassels.*** Sterling Publications: New York 1999.

Makeup, Mehndi and Body Art

Batra, Sumita. ***The Art of Mehndi.*** Penguin: New York 1999.

Camphausen, Rufus. ***Return to the Tribal: A Celebration of Body Adornment.*** Inner Traditions International 1997.

Delamar, Penny. ***The Complete Make-Up Artist: Working in Film, Television and Theatre.*** Northwestern University Press: Chicago 1995.

Fabius, Carine and Michele M. Garcia. ***Mehndi: The Art of Henna Body Painting.*** Three Rivers Printing: Three Rivers, 1998.

Holt, Michael. ***Costume and Make Up (Phaidon Theater Manuals).*** Phaidon Press: New York 1995.

Jans, Martin and William-Alan Landes. ***Stage Make-Up Techniques.*** Players Press: New York 1993.

Miller, Jean-Chris. ***The Body Art Book.*** Berkley Publishing Group: Berkeley 1997.

Roome, Loretta. ***Mehndi: The Timeless Art of Henna Painting.*** Griffin Trade Paperback 1998.

Swinfield, Rosemarie. ***Stage Makeup Step-By-Step: The Complete Guide to Basic Makeup, Planning and Designing Makeup, Adding and Reducing Age, Ethnic Makeup, Special Effects.*** Betterway Publications: Whitehall, VA 1995.

Weinberg, Norma Pasekoff. ***Henna from Head to Toe.*** Storey Books: Pownal, VT 1999.

Clip Art, Design References and Art Historical Sources

Abas, S. J. ***Symmetries of Islamic Geometrical Patterns.*** World Scientific: New Jersey 1995.

Akar, Axade. ***Authentic Turkish Designs.*** Dover Publications: New York 1992.

Akar Azade. ***Treasury of Turkish Designs.*** Dover Publications, Inc.: New York 1988.

Allane, Lee. ***Oriental Rugs: A Buyers Guide.*** Thames and Hudson: London 1988.

Alloula, Malek. ***The Colonial Harem.*** University of Minnesota Press: Minneapolis 1986.

Blackman, Winifred. ***The Fellahin of Upper Egypt.*** G. G. Harrap & Co. Ltd.: London 1927.

Bloom, Jonathan and Sheila S. Blair. ***Islamic Arts.*** Phaidon Press:New York 1997.

Brend, Barbara. ***Islamic Art.*** Harvard University Press: Cambridge, Mass. 1991.

Buourgoin, J. ***Islamic Patterns.*** Dover Publications, Inc.: New York 1978.

Davies, Peter. ***The Tribal Eye: Antique Kilims of Anatolia.*** Rizzoli: New York 1993.

Eastern Encounters: Orientalist Painters of the Nineteenth Century. Fine Art Society, Ltd.: London 1978.

Farooqi, Anis. ***Art of India and Persia.*** D. K. Publishers' Distribuaters: New Delhi 1979.

Gantzhorn, Volkmar. ***Oriental Carpets.*** Taschen: New York 1998.

Grafton, Carol Belanger. ***Egyptian Designs.*** Dover Publications, Inc.: New York 1993.

Hamann, Bradford R. ***The Greek Design Book.*** Stemmer House Publishers: Owings Mills, MA 1980.

Irwin, Robert. ***Islamic Art in Context: Art, Architecture and the Literary World.*** Harry N. Abrams:New York 1997.

Islam in the Balkans: Persian Art and Culture of the 18th and 19th Centuries. Royal Scottish Museum: Edinburgh 1979.

Lewis, Barnard. ***The World of Islam: Faith, People, Culture.*** W. W. Norton & Co.: New York 1992.

Lewis, Reina. ***Gendering Orientalism: Race, Femininity and Representation.*** Routledge: New York 1996.

MacKenzie, John M. ***Orientalism: History, Theory and the Arts.*** Manchester University Press: Manchester 1995.

Pope, Arthur Upham. ***A Survey of Persian Art from Prehistoric Times to the Present.*** Oxford University Press: London 1964-65.

Revault, Jactues. ***Designs & Patterns from North African Carpets & Textiles.*** Dover Publications Inc.: 1973.

Rice, David T. ***Constantinople from Byzantium to Istanbul.*** Stein and Day: New York 1965.

Rice, David T. ***Islamic Art.*** Praeger: New York 1965.

Rogers, J. M. ***Mughal Miniatures.*** Thames and Hudson: London 1993.

Simakoff, N. ***Islamic Designs in Color.*** Dover Publications: New York 1993.

Thompson, James. ***The East, Imagined, Experienced, Remembered: Orientalist Nineteenth Century Painting.*** National Gallery of Ireland: Dublin 1988.

Thornton, Lynne. ***Women as Portrayed in Orientalist Painting.*** ACR Edition: Paris 1985.

Titley, Norah M. ***Persian Painting: Fourteenth Century.*** Marg/Arnold-Heinemann: New Delhi 1977.

Valcarenghi, Dario. ***Kilim: History and Symbols.*** Electa 1994.

Vogel, Lucien. ***Moroccan Silk Designs in Full Color.*** Dover Publications Inc: New York 1996.

Welch, Stuart Cary. ***Persian Painting.*** George Braziller: New York 1996.

Wilson, Eva. ***Ancient Egyptian Designs for Artists and Craftspeople.*** Dover Publications Inc.: New York 1987.

Wilson, Eva. ***Islamic Designs for Artists and Craftspeople.*** Dover Publications: New York 1988.

Hand of Fatima

www.ingramcontent.com/pod-product-compliance
Lightning Source LLC
Chambersburg PA
CBHW080338270326
41927CB00014B/3273
* 9 7 8 0 6 1 5 4 8 8 2 7 1 *